T3-BWO-284

# Blessed Are They

## Exploring Conversion and the Experience of God in Matthew's Gospel

## David M. Knight

**His Way, Inc.**
1310 Dellwood Avenue
Memphis, Tennessee 38127
1985

This book was originally published
under the title FIRST STEPS IN CHRISTIAN DISCIPLESHIP
Dimension Books, 1982

## ACKNOWLEDGEMENTS

Deep thanks to Sister Agnes Stretz, of the Monastery of Saint Clare in Memphis, for typing this manuscript before going to Huehuetenango, Guatemala, to help found there the new Poor Clare Monastery of Our Lady of Wisdom of the Virgin of Guadalupe. To her this book is dedicated, and to the new foundation all its royalties.

# TABLE OF CONTENTS

## INTRODUCTION:

## BELIEVER, TELL ME YOUR HEART

We hear a lot today about the act of accepting Jesus. People are frequently asked, "Have you accepted Jesus in your life? Have you accepted Him as your personal Savior?"

We used to associate this question with the more fundamentalist or evangelical religions. Even today it may suggest to us the "Jesus freaks" or those sects in Christianity which seem to be based more on emotion than on deep understanding of Christ's word. We suspect that for many people "accepting Jesus" has more to do with accepting the support and enthusiasm of a peer group than it does with solid spiritual experience. We see the hand-clapping and the hugging, the laughter and the tears, the shiny sureness and zeal of those who have been "saved," and we wonder how much of this still endures when the guitars have stopped playing and the faith-sharing group has dispersed. We hear the testimonies of instant transformation so confidently delivered by those who have been "born again" or "baptized in the Spirit" and it strikes us as naive. We know from the writings of the mystics and the lives of the Saints how much is really involved in the act of total surrender to God, and how much purification of heart must take place in the process of coming to this surrender. We know this; and because we know it, it pains us to hear people describe, one after another, how in a moment of conversion they "turned their whole lives over to Jesus." We just don't believe it is real.

Our reaction is both right and wrong. The conversions we hear about are real — if not in every case, then in enough instances to make the phenomenon something we have to take seriously. Young people are leaving the older, more established religions to join shaky sects of a few years' flashy existence which, like shooting stars, suddenly appear out of nowhere and will probably disappear just as suddenly into nothingness. But there is no questioning the fact that the lives of these young people have been changed. They have been given a new vision of hope, a new experience of life and of relatedness to God, a set of ideals that are real and inspiring to them, and the strength and support they need — both inner and outer — to live by them. And they do beautiful things. Their lives, whether deeply or shallowly, are rooted in love (see *Ephesians* 3:17).

The movement back to Jesus is not confined to the young. Older people — adults in their thirties and forties, people whose children have grown up and gone to college, men and women established in business and family life — have had deep conversion experiences that have changed the whole tone and level of their spiritual lives. In the examples of this that I have known, the conversion did not usually involve a change of religion, but rather an affiliation with some group within their own denomination — a prayer group, a study group, or a nationwide (and international) movement such as the Charismatic

Renewal, the Cursillo or Marriage Encounter. Clearly, conversion is taking place, and it is a phenomenon that must be reckoned with. What does it say to us?

What this phenomenon has said to me is that there is something missing in our understanding of religion. An important growth-step of the Christian life is being overlooked, both in the pastoral approach of the clergy and lay ministers, and in the expectations of those who look upon themselves as just being sheep in the flock. Our churches are like huge engines in which the gasoline is brought again and again into the combustion chamber, lifted up to the sparkplugs, and never ignited. The spark isn't there. After thousands of trips through this cycle, over years of church attendance, many Christians either just drain quietly out of the system or resign themselves to keep going indefinitely through the motions, but without any hope that their spiritual lives will ever catch fire.

Others get ignited — "turned on" — by the sects, the cults, the flash-in-the-pan evangelical preachers, and burn out in one quick undirected blaze like gasoline spread over the grass. Either way it is a waste of the world's most precious potential: the potential of the human heart to know and respond to God.

I believe that what is lacking (among other things) in our understanding of religion is a clear recognition of the need every Christian has, at some point in his or her spiritual life, to make a conscious, explicit, radical and affective act of acceptance of Jesus Christ.

This act of acceptance was made, for most of us, by other people who answered in our name when we were baptized as infants. As we grew up we ratified the commitment they had made in our name; we accepted without revolt to follow the religion we were brought up in. And this acceptance was real. The light of faith had been given to us at baptism, and so we found little difficulty believing in the truth we were taught. The fire of divine love had actually been enkindled in our hearts with the gift of the Holy Spirit at baptism, and so we found ourselves able, almost without effort, perhaps, to live by the ideals of Jesus Christ as we understood them. Or if we didn't live by these ideals, at least we acknowledged them as our own — to the extent, at least, of nor formally renouncing them — and in the back of our minds we had the idea that someday we might look at them more closely and perhaps try to live them as they deserved to be lived.

This was a real acceptance of Jesus. It just wasn't very conscious, very explicit, very personal, very radical, or very clear. It was like the acceptance we gave to being American: we had no reason to become anything else, so we went along, more or less, with what we were expected to do. We might say that our acceptance of Christianity, like our acceptance of the American way of life, was less a choice of Christianity itself than an absence of reason for choosing anything else. We found what we were acceptable and had no incentive to change. We remained Christians by inertia.

I don't want to make this sound worse than it was. Positive inertia can be a powerful force. It is inertia which keeps the satellites in orbit. Once an object is launched into motion, its tendency is to keep moving forever. Theoretically, if it met with no resistance at all it would just never stop. And baptism was a powerful launching of our spiritual lives, our lives of grace. Not only that, but if the Christian community we grew up in — family, parish, Church — was a live and dynamic one, we probably picked up more and more momentum in our spiritual lives just through the forward motion of the community. Objectively speaking, we may have been living the life of grace on a very high level of performance all our lives, carried by the inertia of our baptism and the momentum of the Christian community in which we were brought up. But that doesn't mean we were on fire.

The ignition point in our spiritual lives comes when we consciously, explicitly, and radically accept Jesus Christ as the person on whom and on whose teachings we intend to base our whole existence. When I say this I do not mean to imply, as the first two chapters of this book will make clear, that this has to take place in a single, dramatic moment. For many people it does happen this way, but more often, I believe, it does not. But it has to happen. And we have to know, in a clear and conscious way, that it has happened.

What is more, for this acceptance of Jesus to be effective in our lives and a source of continuing power and growth, we have to have some sharp, scientific understanding about what acceptance of Jesus implies. We have to know, in a practical way that translates easily into action, what acceptance of Jesus means.

This book does not have as its goal to spell out in concrete detail the changes that acceptance of Jesus should make in our daily life. I hope to do so in a later book on discipleship and the Sermon on the Mount — a book that asks, "What difference does it make to be Christian?" In this book my goal is only to clarify two things: first, it is to make clear what the act of accepting Jesus really is — what it means to experience "conversion." And secondly, to establish the fundamental platform of attitudes and values on which our continuing response to Jesus must be built. This book deals with what happens *inside of us* when we make a "decision for Jesus." It doesn't focus on what happens inside of us emotionally, but on the response of intellect and will, of faith and understanding and commitment which must take place for our acceptance of Jesus to be authentic and complete.

I believe that the great majority of the conversions we see around us — the emotional, naive, enthusiastic and beautiful "decisions for Jesus" (by whatever name they may be called from one group to another) that characterize the anti-intellectual and non-traditional bubble-groups of Christianity — are real conversions: sincere and authentic responses to grace. But I also believe that in most cases these conversions are unenlightened, misdirected and incomplete as acts of acceptance of Jesus. That conversion has taken place is indisputable. That this conversion is, in some way, to Jesus is usually equally clear. But that this conversion is an authentic acceptance of Jesus in the sense that it contains within itself everything that real acceptance of Jesus should contain, that is open to much doubt. And that is a tragedy.

The real problem, however, is not in the "conversions to Jesus" that are inviable or crippled. The real problem, the problem we have to face, is the absence — or the invisibility, perhaps — of a clear, conscious and radical acceptance of Jesus by the great  body of believers who attend the established churches every Sunday, and whose own enthusiasm, or lack of it, is the only evident face of orthodox Christian religion. By enthusiasm, of course, I don't mean just emotion. I mean a real and radical acceptance of Jesus that is carried out into action, transforming all human life and behavior.

It is this acceptance of Jesus which is the subject of this book and which will, I hope, be brought into conscious completeness and vigor in the hearts of all who read it.

## CHAPTER ONE

## ACCEPTING THE CALL TO CONVERSION

Jesus the Teacher begins by addressing our whole being. The truth He teaches is truth to be responded to. It is not just truth to receive with our minds; it is truth to embrace with our wills and carry our physically into action. It calls our whole being to life.

 To accept Jesus, then, is to change interiorly in a radical way. It is to become different and to act differently. This is "conversion."

In the Gospel of Matthew this condition for response to Jesus' teaching is established before Jesus Himself even begins to preach. The first words of John the Baptizer, who prepares the way for Him, are "Reform your lives! The reign of God is at hand" *(Matthew* 3:1-2).

Reform. *Metanoeite.* The word is translated sometimes as "repent," sometimes as "reform your lives." Its basic meaning is a "change of mind." What John is preaching and Jesus will preach after him (see *Matthew* 4:17), is a change of attitudes and values, a fundamental change of direction in life. This change takes place interiorly, in the mind and heart and will, and manifests itself exteriorly in a change of behavior.

*12*

John doesn't just say "Reform." He also says, "Give some *evidence* that you mean to reform" *(Matthew 3:8).* Let the "word" of your decision take flesh in your actions.

Acceptance of Jesus takes place in an act of interior conversion which must be embodied in external actions to be complete. To understand what it means to accept Jesus, we need to look more closely at what this act of conversion is.

### An active choice on our part

The "good news" about this call to conversion is that in the very act of saving us through Jesus, God takes our humanity seriously. Jesus doesn't come to save us like pieces of inert matter. He calls us to action: to choice, to decision, to self-determination. It is not our behavior alone that Jesus saves; it is *us;* our free, personal, choosing selves. What He comes to redeem is our freedom, the core of our personhood. And He redeems our freedom by calling it to response.

Jesus shows His power precisely in calling on us to change. If He did not — if He somehow just "made us good" by a one-sided act of power (as we in our short-sightedness sometimes beg Him to do) — He would not be taking us seriously, not be redeeming our humanity. He would not be saving the persons that we are, and the process of free, self-determining self-creation which is the essence of created personhood, but He would be "taking over" and doing for us the one thing which it is our human dignity to do for ourselves: namely, choosing what we will believe with our minds, what we will embrace with our wills, what we will actually carry out into action and do. If Jesus just took away the evil in us and made us good, He would not be saving *us,* but substituting for our own personalities some other reality — manufactured afresh in heaven and dropped into our bodies or our hearts — but not a personality of our own free making.

Christian conversion, then, is something that Jesus does not do for us. He makes it possible for us to do it by acts of our own freedom. He does it with us and in us, but He doesn't do it for us. As a result, the person we become through our conversion to Him is truly us, the result of our own free self-determination. We are what we are because it is what we have freely chosen to be. And this ability to create ourselves, our persons, by acts of free choice is the very essence of our likeness to God.

## Characteristics of the act of acceptance

The first characteristic of this conversion is *awareness.* Whatever change takes place in our attitudes and values, it must be a free, personal act. Christian conversion is not cultural conditioning or subtle manipulation or brainwashing. It is the exact opposite of numb, unthinking conformity. For our conversion to Christ to be real and acceptable to God, we must know that we are choosing. Authentic Christian conversion makes us aware of our freedom and of ourselves as free and choosing persons. It is an entrance into possession of our personhood; into conscious self-identity. Jesus will say later that through conversion to Him we "discover who we are" (see *Matthew* 10:30, *New American Bible* translation).

For this one doesn't have to go through some dramatic "conversion experience." A Baptist mis-

sionary in Africa once asked me when I had been
"saved." I told him I couldn't attach any date to that
moment except the date of my baptism as an infant.
In my own experience God had always been real to
me. I grew up believing in Jesus and accepting Him as
Savior and Lord. The minister's experience had been
different: he had first consciously recognized and
accepted Jesus as an adult, when during a revival he
walked up to the altar and put his life in His hands.
To my surprise, the minister's wife said she had
experienced salvation the way I had: she had grown
up believing in Jesus; she had always taken Him for
real in her life, and couldn't say when it began.

Acceptance of Jesus must be conscious. It must
be personal, and deep, and not just a part of one's
social identification with others. We don't accept
Jesus because our family does, or because it is taken
for granted in the church we grew up in. Such a
response to Jesus would really be nothing but an
acceptance of other people, of their attitudes and
behavior, and not a true relationship with the person
of Jesus. But our conscious acceptance of Jesus need
not take place in a dramatic moment. For many
people it does — and when this happens it is a
moment of grace. But the essential is to know that we
are deliberately walking in His light, no matter how
or when we become aware that the light is there and
that we believe it is His. For this a gradual dawning is
just as much an experience of God as a lightning bolt
is.

*"Give some evidence . . . "*

A second characteristic of Christian conversion
is that it is *expressed in action.* This is what makes it

"real." We don't actually know whether our
acceptance of Jesus is real or not until we see it
expressed and embodied in our choices. And no
interior "word" of choice is fully real until it "takes
flesh" in action. That is why John the Baptizer
insisted with his listeners, "Give some evidence that
you mean to reform." In the eyes of God — and in our
own eyes too — our words have only the value of our
actions. Until we begin to *act* differently in response
to the words and example of Jesus we can't be sure
that His words and example have reached us. Until
He affects the way we live, we do not have the
experience of knowing Him as truly real to us. Unless
we can "bring forth fruit appropriate to conversion" it
is hard for us to be convinced that we have taken
Christ for real.

## *"The ax is laid to the root . . . "*

If our conversion is to Jesus, it must be *radical;*
that is, it must get down to the roots of our life and of
our choices: to the deep attitudes, values, goals and
orientation out of which our day-to-day choices grow.
John says, "The ax is laid to the root of the tree."
Change the root and all the fruit changes. Change the
basic orientation, intentionality, or goal of a person's
life and everything that person does will change.

That is what St. Paul experienced, and what he
was talking about when he wrote:

> But those things I used to consider gain I have now
> reappraised as loss in the light of Christ. I have come
> to rate all as loss in the light of the surpassing
> knowledge of my Lord Jesus Christ. For his sake I
> have forfeited everything; I have accounted all else
> rubbish so that Christ may be my wealth . . .
>
> *(Philippians* 3:7-8)

This is the only level of conversion that is worthy of Jesus Christ. He did not come to "touch things up" a little bit on earth; He came to turn things upside down, to make all things new (see *Isaiah* 43:19; 1 *Corinthians* 5:7; *Revelation* 21:5). He came to have the impact on this world that a hundred and twenty gallons of wine had on the tiny country wedding reception in Cana (see *John* 2:1-11). The event of Jesus' coming and the message of His Gospel have put all human life on a different footing. Until, like St. Paul, we have recognized this, our conversion to Christ is not complete and our acceptance is not worthy of Him. Until our response to Jesus has penetrated to the very roots of all our thoughts, actions and desires on earth, it has not reached its natural depth.

## Key areas of response

The choices, then, and the external actions which express our conversion to Christ must involve the root values of our existence: money, sex, power, human relationships, achievement, basic life securities. Jesus mentions all of these: "If you seek  perfection [which means, in context, just "if you want to be a Christian" — see *Jerome Biblical Commentary:* 43:134, on *Matthew* 19:21 (Prentice Hall, 1968)] go, sell your possessions, and give to the poor" *(Matthew* 19:21). When He gave His scandalous teaching on divorce Jesus said, "Some there are who have freely renounced sex for the sake of God's reign. Let him accept this teaching who can" *(Matthew* 19:12). To His disciples ambitious for power He said, "You know how those who exercise authority among the Gentiles lord it over them; their great ones make their importance felt. It cannot be like that with you. Anyone among you who aspires to greatness must serve the rest" *(Matthew* 20:25-26).

Jesus challenged the supremacy of our most sacred human relationships when He said, "Whoever loves father or mother, son or daughter, more than me is not worthy of me" *(Matthew* 10:37). He called into question our basic assumptions about achievement when He taught us to value our relationship with God more than our ability to perform *(Luke* 10:20); the intention in our hearts more than our accomplishments *(Luke* 21:3-4); and the simple fact of being allowed to serve God more than the reward we receive for it *(Matthew* 20:1-16). He called on those who would believe in Him to prove it by abandoning all concern about fundamental human securities: food and clothing *(Matthew* 6:25 ff.); shelter *(Matthew* 8:20); means of livelihood *(Matthew* 4:20, 22); even life itself *(Matthew* 10:28-33).

Conversion to Jesus must be radical. It isn't a matter of trimming the leaves and branches of our lives to make a good appearance; the ax must be laid to the root. The change in us must take place on that deep level of our being where all of our desires and choices originate. It must touch our personal roots.

### A growing gift of self

Fortunately, this doesn't have to happen all at once. It is comforting to see that John the Baptizer answers with very ordinary, down-to-earth things when the crowds cry out to him, "What ought we to do?" (see *Luke* 3:10 ff.). Those who have more than they absolutely need should share with those who have not *(Luke* 3:11). Those whose business or profession inclines them to take cheating for granted should simply be honest *(Luke* 3:12-13). Those who are in a position to use power for personal gain should refuse to do so *(Luke* 3:14). Later, Jesus will translate the radical response He calls for into concrete demands that are more and more challenging (see the examples above). But acceptance of Him and His Gospel, like everything else that is human, is a live and growing thing. And like all live things, it begins small.

## *Awareness and expression*

We must not miss the connection that exists between interior conversion and its external expression. The only way we can be deeply and convincingly *aware* of our conversion to Christ is to *express* our conversion in action. And the only way we can know that our conversion to Him is radical is to express it in radical actions.

Abraham received a promise from God (see *Genesis,* ch. 12 ff.). The promise meant a great deal to him, because it spelled the difference between a fulfilled life and an existence which was ultimately meaningless. In Abraham's case, the issue was posterity. He lived in a rather primitive society that provided little opportunity for individuation. About the only way to "stand out," to distinguish oneself from the other members of the tribe and find self-identity, was to raise goats. There wasn't much art, technology or politics. To be somebody meant to build up an impressive flock of sheep and goats with which to feed a large number of helpers, wives and dependents. As the leader of all these people, a man could have power and prestige. And Abraham was on the way to acquiring all this.

The trouble was, he had no children. This meant that when he died, all his sheep and goats — and all his individuality, therefore — would just be divided up among his followers. The "name" of Abraham would cease to exist. All his built-up self-identity would be forfeit. And Abraham said as much to God: "O Lord God, what good will your gifts be, if I keep on being childless . . . ? See, you have given me no offspring, and so one of my servants will be my heir" *(Genesis* 15:2-3).

Then God made His great promise to Abraham: "Look up at the sky and count the stars, if you can. Just so shall your descendants be: as numerous as the stars in the sky and the sands of the seashore" (see *Genesis* 15:5; *Hebrews* 11:12).

But how did Abraham know this promise was real? His first reaction to it was to laugh *(Genesis* 17:17), and when his wife Sarah heard the news, she laughed even more *(Genesis* 18:12-15). How did Abraham know he wasn't dreaming, or that he hadn't added his own interpretation to something else God was communicating to him in prayer?

If God had left it at that, Abraham would not have had to know. He could have taken the position, "Maybe God spoke to me, maybe not. Maybe I will have children, maybe not. Who knows? If the promise turns out to be true, so much the better. If not, I'm no worse off than I was before." But God didn't leave it at that.

The very first thing God said to Abraham was, "Go forth from the land of your kinsfolk and from your father's house to a land that I will show you" *(Genesis* 12:1). In other words, if you want me to give you ultimate meaning in life (as you understand it — that is, to give you an heir), *leave* everything that makes your life meaningful here and now. Leave your country, your kinsfolk, and your father's house. Show your faith in My promise by an act of radical response.

For a primitive, nomad tribesman, there was nothing else of value to leave. His tribal grazing lands, the bonds and the support of clan and family, these were all that gave security and a human level of existence on earth. And God told Abraham to leave them.

His pedagogy is clear: Abraham would never have had to decide whether he believed in God's promise or not unless he staked something on it — something as proportionately precious to him as the promise itself. Until he *expressed* his faith through some real and radical gesture of unambiguous belief, Abraham could not really know whether he believed or not. It was the *risk of his response* that made him aware of himself as a believer. He knew the radicalness of his conversion through the radicalness of his response. From the moment he left his country, his kinsfolk, and his father's house, Abraham knew himself as a man who walked in covenanted relationship with God.

## Unambiguous response

For our acceptance of Christ to be authentic and complete it must not only be radical; it must also be *unambiguous*. That is, it must be an act that doesn't make sense — one that cannot be explained — except as a response of graced faith, hope and love given to the person of Jesus Christ and His message.

There are many reasons to be a Christian besides belief in Jesus Christ. In some societies church membership provides status, or at least a certain acceptance and belonging. For many people being a "Christian" is just synonymous with being a decent, conservative, neighborly human being.[1] For those who approve of basic Christian ethics, as these are understood in our society, and who find churchgoing pleasant or even inspirational, it doesn't take any real faith to be a member of a church. People in this category might go to church their whole lives long, and keep all the rules of their religion, without ever knowing — in any deep or personal way, at least — whether they believe in Jesus Christ at all.

Real acceptance of Jesus is an unambiguous act of faith. It involves taking a stance toward this world — i.e., toward its real values, toward benefits that are tangible and concrete — which simply does not make sense without belief in the teaching of the Gospel. Unambiguous converstion to Jesus Christ means living twenty-four hours a day in such a way that our choices do not make sense without Him.[2]

*"The Holy Spirit and fire . . . "*

A conversion on this level is obviously impossible without grace. By definition a Christian conversion is a conversion, not to just good, reasonable, moral human behavior, but to a way of thinking, judging and acting which is *proper to God alone.* That is why John the Baptizer told the people who listened to his moral exhortations, "I baptize you in water for the sake of reform, but the one who will follow me is more powerful than I . . . He it is who will baptize you in the Holy Spirit and fire" *(Matthew* 3:11). Christian conversion is an elightenment of the mind to see things as God sees them, and an enlivening of the will to love as God loves by the gift of the Holy Spirit who has been poured out in our hearts (see *Romans* 5:5).

We receive this gift of the Spirit and of new life by being made one with Jesus Christ as members of His Body. This is an act of God which changes our whole level of being.

The baptism which expresses our conversion is not just a human act. It is not just an expression of our human choice. It is an act of God. By this act we are mystically incorporated into Christ. In the act of our baptism we become members of Him, members of the body which died on the cross and rose. Thus the act of being baptized is an act which trandscends time, an act of dying "in Christ" in the body that hung on the cross two thousand years ago, and simultaneously an act of rising "in Christ" to live now on earth as members of His risen Body. Because we live and act "in Him," we are able to act on the level of God's own knowing and loving. The divine life of Christ is our life; His Spirit is united to our spirit, and through His light and power and life we find ourselves able to respond to God and to human situations with a faith, a hope, a love which surpass all human knowing and ability to give. This is what it means to be baptized "in the Holy Spirit and fire."

*Drawing hope from an event*

The *motivating force* of Christian conversion, then, is an *event.* "Reform your lives," John preaches, because "the reign of God is at hand" *(Matthew* 3:2). The starting point, the exciting force of the whole drama of Christian life in the world is the coming of

Jesus Christ. Because He has come; because He has begun His reign and broken the power of sin on earth; because it is possible now for us to be united to Him in grace and to share His light and life, the radical transformation of Christian conversion is possible. Christ's coming is an event with a promise: "He will baptize you in the Holy Spirit and fire." We initiate our process of change because God has drawn near to us, to invite us, to encourage us and give us power and hope.

The Gospel is the "good news," not the good advice. Good advice is something a person is left with to follow if he can. Moral exhortations and wise counselling are good advice. But the good news of the Gospel is something that gives us new hope: a hope based, not on what we are able to do of ourselves, even with expert coaching, but on an intervention of God in history, in our own lives. And the name of this intervention is "Jesus," which means "God saves."[3]

### Confession of sins — profession of faith

There are two other points to notice about conversion as it appears in the preaching of John the Baptizer. First, it typically begins with a *confession of sins* (see *Matthew* 3:6).

We should not interpret this confession as some kind of psychological grovelling in guilt or wallowing in self-accusation. We know from Jesus' own description of reconciliation that God does not put a lot of emphasis on a detailed enumeration of faults. In the story of the Prodigal Son the father doesn't even allow the boy to finish his carefully-rehearsed speech of self-accusation and apology. He interrupts him before he finishes and calls for the servants to bring out the robe and the ring and the fatted calf for the feasting (see *Luke* 15:18-24).

The confession of sins appropriate to Christian conversion is in reality an admission of sins whose purpose is to be a *profession* of ideals. We make explicit what we *reject* as sin in order to make clear what we *accept* as the authentic norm of our behavior. Recognizing that our conduct has cast some doubt on our ideals, we profess our ideals again by confessing our departures from them as something we ourselves condemn as wrong.

This profession is a profession of *faith*. Christian conversion is not just from the bad to the good. It is from the god to the Godlike. What the Christian turns away from in the act of "converting" or of "turning to" Christ is not just that level of behavior which all human beings should recognize as "bad" — the evil acts of exploitation, violence, oppression, deceitfulness, etc. — but *all* behavior which is not according to to the mind and heart, the attitudes and values, of Jesus Christ Himself. St. Paul instructs us to let our *faith* be our rule of life *(Romans* 14:22), and faith is simply union of mind with Christ Himself, a sharing in the light of His own knowledge.[4] To be converted to Christ is to be "transformed by the renewal of your mind" *(Romans* 12:2). It is to put on the "mind of Christ" (2 *Corinthians* 2:16) and "acquire a fresh, spiritual way of thinking" *(Ephesians* 4:24). Authentic acceptance of Jesus can be nothing less than this.

What "confession of sin" means, then, in an act of Christian conversion is that we profess before God and man to have embraced in faith the teaching, the ideals, of Jesus Christ; we have received and accepted His light as the light by which we evaluate all human decisions. It means that in the light of what we *now* see and accept as the ideal of graced behavior, we acknowledge that our former ideals and behavior have "fallen short." Like St. Paul we say "those things I used to consider gain I have now *reappraised* as loss *in the light of Christ"* (Philippians 3:7). In other words, every Christian confession of sin is a profession of higher ideals. Christian conversion is an upgrading of our moral standards; and not a human or personal upgrading only, but an acceptance of and surrender to the standards of Jesus Himself. If in our confession of sin we "look down on" the way we acted before, this is only possible because in some way — at least in values and desire — we have already risen above it. The essential element in this confession of sins is not that we condemn our past actions as bad, but that by doing so we profess our acceptance of the ideals of Jesus as good. We accept to be judged and to judge ourselves by His standards rather than by whatever measure or values we used before. This is a profession of faith.

### Change the root — change the fruit

It follows that Christian conversion must be *fruitful*. It should manifest itself in a level of behavior that is obviously the fruit of graced union with Jesus Christ, life according to the Spirit. John the Baptizer declared, "Every tree that is not fruitful will be cut down . . . " John called on his hearers to bring forth fruit "worthy of repentance." But Jesus goes further than this: the fruit He calls for is the fruit of branches vitally one with the vine. He is the vine, and the fruit of those who are one with Him must be fruit worthy of Jesus Himself:

Live on in me, as I do in you.
No more than a branch can bear fruit of itself
apart from the vine,
can you bear fruit
apart from me.

I am the vine, you are the branches.
He who lives in me and I in him,
will produce abundantly,
for apart from me you can do nothing.

*(John* 15:4-5)

It is here that the unambiguously Christian character of our conversion should appear. For us to be aware that we have indeed encountered and responded to the grace of Jesus Christ, it is not enough that our conversion be expressed in actions. The actions themselves must be such that they could have no other source — for us subjectively, at least — than a true, interior grasp and deep, personal acceptance of the attitudes and values of Christ. For our behavior to bear witness to grace, our choices must reveal the active, speaking presence of the Holy Spirit in our hearts and show that we are listening to Him and acting by His power as branches united to the vine.

This is the kind of conversion to which Jesus calls us as "Master of the Way." And this is the kind of conversion it takes for us to truly accept Him as He is.

### FOOTNOTES

[1]See the discussion of this in my book *His Way,* chapter six: "Connecting Christianity with Life: How to Get to Florida by Way of California" (St. Anthony Messenger Press, 1977).

[2]For a development of how the daily life of lay Christians in the world can be an experience of real, radical, unambiguous response to the Gospel, see my book *Lift Up Your Eyes To The*

*Mountain,* chapter eight: "How To Be An Ordinary Mystic" (Dimension Books, 1981).

[3]Readers may want to refer to the explanation of salvation and of Jesus as Savior in chapters four and five of my earlier book: *Questions for Today: WHY JESUS?* (Dimension Books, 1981).

[4]See *Questions for Today: WHY JESUS?* chapter eight, for an explanation of faith in these terms.

## CHAPTER ONE: ACCEPTING THE CALL TO CONVERSION — *Matthew* 3:1-12

Summary:

1. Acceptance of Jesus implies a *conversion:* an interior change of attitudes, values and goals expressed externally in a change of behavior. In requiring active choices on our part, God takes our humanity seriously.

2. Acceptance of Jesus is characterized by *awareness* as a free and conscious response to the person of Jesus. It must be *expressed in action* to be fully real. It must be *radical,* involving a conversion at the roots of our motivation and goals, from which our choices receive their orientation. And it must be *unambiguously* a response of faith, hope and love to Jesus Christ and His Gospel.

3. Christian conversion is motivated by the *event* of Christ's coming, and is based on *hope* in the power of His grace. It is a conversion, not only from the bad to the good, but specifically from the good to the Godlike: to a level of operation and behavior proper to God alone, to which we are raised only by participating in God's own nature by grace. It must reveal itself in actions which can only be the fruit of a real and living union with Christ through responsiveness to the Holy Spirit who dwells in our hearts.

4. Conversion to Christ typically begins with a *confession of sins* which is in reality a *profession* of faith in the attitudes and values, the truth and ideals of Jesus. To accept Jesus we must accept to "put on the mind of Christ" and judge our behavior henceforth by His standards.

*Questions for prayer and discussion:*

1. Has anything led you to believe that by "accepting Jesus" you would be instantly transformed interiorly, and all your temptations and difficulties would disappear? If it did

happen this way, would that be something you would want? How would you feel afterwards, in heaven, about yourself and your love for God?

2. When did you first become aware that you believed in Jesus and took Him seriously? Do you sense in the presence of most of the Christians you know that they are aware of relating personally in faith, hope and love to Jesus Christ? Do you feel this awareness among the people you go to church with? What concrete, sensible signs make you feel this awareness does or does not exist in your friends? In your church community?

3. What real, concrete actions or choices in your life express your acceptance of Jesus Christ? Your conversion to the ideals and values of His Gospel? What choices show that your acceptance of Jesus has changed the goal and motivation of your life at its roots? What do you do that is unambiguously a response to Jesus Christ — i.e., that could not (in your case, at least) be motivated by anything else but faith and hope and love placed in Him?

4. When you confess your sins, do you experience this as a deep, personal profession of acceptance of the ideals and values of Jesus Christ? Do you judge your behavior by His standards or by the accepted practices of your peer group? Where do you look in order to discover the values of Jesus?

## CHAPTER TWO

## THE EXPERIENCE OF
## RELATEDNESS TO GOD

The first fruit of authentic Christian conversion is an experience of relatedness to God. Thus the act of accepting Jesus is also an experience of being accepted by Him. When we "convert" to Christianity we don't just decide to live and act in a different way; we accept Jesus as our Savior and Teacher of life. We decide to base our lives on relationship with Him: on faith in His teaching, hope in His power and help, love for what He is and can be for us.

But our acceptance of Jesus might come to mature awareness only gradually, through many small acts of limited "conversion." Each time we decide to do good — as Jesus defines it, and because we believe in Him — instead of doing whatever else we may be inclined to do, we are "converting" to His message and to His person more deeply. Each one of these small and perhaps hardly noticed "conversions" is an experience — also small and perhaps hardly noticed — of relatedness to Him. Every time we make a choice based on faith in Him, every time we take seriously His right to rule and guide us in our life, we are experiencing our relatedness to Jesus in the act of another small "conversion" to His way.

The very structure of Matthew's Gospel brings out this connection between the act or choice of conversion and the experience of relatedness to God. After describing the call to conversion in John the Baptizer's preaching, the next scene Matthew puts before us in Jesus' own symbolic gesture of conversion: His decision to be baptized by John at the Jordan river (see *Matthew* 3:13-17). And this is followed by a profound experience of God. The heavens are opened and Jesus hears the Father saying, "This is my beloved Son."

Jesus was not in need of conversion. But His gesture of accepting John's baptism has a double significance:

## Baptism "into" the human race

First, it was a formal — we might even say a theological — expression of what the Incarnation was all about. When Jesus became man, God truly became one with the human race: one of us, a part of our history, a part of all we are. When Jesus was baptized, He expressed His own, personal acceptance of this solidarity with the whole of sinful humanity. He was, so to speak, baptized into our human sinfulness just as we, later on, would be baptized into His divine innocence. Jesus had no sin; He had no need of repentance for sin, no need of forgiveness. When He accepted for Himself the baptism that belonged to sinners, instead of being "baptized out of" sin, He was baptized *into* it. His real "baptism" into the human race took place at His Incarnation, of course. But through this gesture at the Jordan He was baptized visibly and symbolically "into" us, and into all our sinful history, just as each of us would be baptized later and in a real way "into Christ," and into His victory over sin: His crucifixion and rising from the dead (see *Romans* 6:3-4).

This sets the pattern of our own baptism: our acceptance of Jesus is an acceptance of solidarity, of oneness, with Him in His act of dying offered on the cross, and in His rising to carry on His mission through the members of His body on earth until the end of time. Christ's baptism was an acceptance of solidarity with us. Our baptism is an acceptance of solidarity with Him.

A second reason for this baptism was for Jesus to set us an example. As "Master of the Way" He led the way. He Himself first made the public gesture of conversion that He would ask of His followers. And so our acceptance of Jesus also should take place in a public act of conversion, through which we give ourselves to Him and to the new way of life that He teaches.

### An experience of God

In response to Jesus' symbolic gesture of conversion, the heavens were opened, and Jesus saw the Spirit of God descend like a dove upon Him. At the same time He heard the Father's voice saying, "This is my beloved Son. My favor rests on Him" *(Matthew* 3:16-17).

This calls our attention to the fact that every authentic conversion is an *experience of God.* And this experience is an experience of *relatedness.*

When we hear the phrase "experience of God," we tend to think in terms of some dramatic, emotional moment of special illumination or feeling. We think of an "experience of God" as something we *receive* rather than *do*. An experience of God is something in the area of mysticism, and God either bestows it on us or He doesn't.

There is truth in this, of course. Every experience of grace is an experience of gift; it is receptivity. But we are wrong in assuming that the experience of God is necessarily dramatic, emotional, or even that it is always noticed! Our experience of God can be like our experience of the sun: we can walk in His light, take comfort in His warmth, and hardly ever advert to the fact that He is there. And yet He is real to us. There are many people who are not aware of ever "experiencing" a sunrise, and yet the sun may be more of a constant reality to them that it is to those who at some particular moment have been awestruck by its beauty and grandeur.

What is essential to the experience of God is not that we should be able on some conscious, explicit occasion to say with deep feeling, "I am experiencing God!" The essential is simply that we should know He is real to us from the fact that we *take Him for real.* Someone who has never experienced electric shock but who is extremely careful around exposed wires can say that electricity is real to him. The same is true of someone who works hard for money although he has never been rich. Anything that determines our choices and affects our life is real to us and we have vivid experience of it. God is no exception to this rule.

This is why every authentic Christian conversion is an experience of God. The heavens do not need to open. We do not need to hear the Father's voice. But whenever we consciously choose in faith to take seriously the reality of Jesus Christ and to base our

conduct on His teaching, we experience our relatedness to God.

### A question of motivation

The kind of relatedness we experience depends
on the motivation of our choice. If we choose, for
example, not to sin on some given occasion because
we are afraid of the punishment of God, we experience ourselves relating to God as creature to Creator,
(or we know ourselves as persons acknowledging
conscience who recognize God as having authority
over us). If, on the other hand, we choose to do
something — to pray trustingly for help, for example
— because Jesus has taught us to call God our Father,
then in the act of making that choice we experience
ourselves as children of the Father.

### Experience of God — experience of choice

That experience of God which comes to us
embodied in the choices we make is a more solid,
more lasting, and more dependable experience of God
than the kind we associate with visions and ecstasies.
Consistent actions performed in faith, simply because
we choose to believe (and find ourselves *able* to
choose to believe, which is the experience of grace),
even if they come without any felt experience of
illumination or any tingling sense of God's reality and
closeness, are a more valid experience of God than
dramatic, emotional happenings. It is a common
principle among spiritual directors that subjective
enlightenments, exaltations and raptures, no matter
how extraordinary, are not to be trusted as authentic

experiences of God unless they show as their fruit some increase of faith, hope and love in our choices. The choices are the key. This is our Lord's own principle: "By their fruits you shall know them" *(Matthew* 7:15-23).

I am not denying, of course, that God can give us enlightenment or movements of grace which we refuse to act upon. But in such a case our experience of God is not complete. His action never comes to term. Soom even the memory of His movement within us will be obscure; it will fade into that vague backdrop of questionable realities which form the unfocused horizon of our experience.

Choices are different. They are the foundation on which we stand. Our choices are our real experience of life — or of ourselves responding to life, which is the same thing. And the experience of God which is embodied in our choices is the experience of God which we live by, build on, use to direct our lives. God is as real to us as the choices in which we respond to Him; no more, no less.

Paradoxically, we may experience God's reality to us in choices that refuse Him — refuse Him but do not ignore Him. If in our choices to sin, for example, we are aware, whether dimly or keenly, that we are choosing to go against the reality of God, that reality becomes more vividly a fact of our experience. For many of us, God may have become "real" — that is, personally, experientially real — for the first time only when we sinned. We chose to act as if He were not there and we discovered that for us He very definitely was. We may have gone on sinning, but we knew we were sinning, not just against values or other people (our parents, for example), but against Him. In our choices we knew He was real.

A Catholic cousin of mine had a drinking buddy — a non-believer — who used to comment on how religious he was.

"Why do you keep saying I'm so religious?" my cousin asked; "I do everything you do."

"I know," his friend replied, "but it bothers you!"

I think the most common — and strongest — Christian experience of God takes place over a period of years, almost without being noticed. This experience lies latent, like unmined ore, in a series of choices based on faith in God's reality, in His presence, His words, His action through the Church; choices that we could not and would not make if God were not acting in us by grace. The choice to pray on our own time and in our own way; the choice not to sin, even when no one will know about it; the choice to take part in the Sunday celebration with personal attention and involvement, even when there is very little "celebration" about it to turn us on; the choice to receive the sacraments believingly and seriously in the deep, quiet solitude of our own hearts — all these choices, repeated over a period of years, form a true, solid foundation of experience of God which is real. As we look back on them we know that God is, and (perhaps for as long as we remember) always has been real to us. We know that our lives have been lived in relationship to Him; that He has been a part of them. We also know that He has been acting in our hearts. Nothing else can explain the way we have responded to Him.

Every authentic experience of God that comes to term, to completion, is then an experience of "conversion." Conversion just means a "turning to" God with belief, decision, and the determination to act. In turning to God we are also "turning away" from anything we perceive at the moment as being in opposition to Him, or at least to this present act of response. Not all conversions are total of course; some are even quite consciously reserved. There was true, if limited, conversion in the prayer of St. Augustine: "Lord, make me chaste — but not yet!" And all of us, if we are honest, know that there are some things we still hold back from God. More than likely, our conversion to Him cannot be complete until we see Him face to face and He wins us entirely with the total beauty of His love.

And conversely, it is in the act of converting to God that we experience relatedness to Him. In our choices to take Him for real (and sometimes in our choices not to) we experience His reality to us.

The basic ingredients, then, of a Christian experience of God are:

1. a true, free, personal choice on our part: "Jesus . . . appeared before John at the Jordan to be baptized by him";

2. which is, in fact, an act of response to grace: to God acting on — and in — our hearts through His word, his Spirit, through the gift of His life shared with us in faith, in hope, in love: "Jesus answered . . . 'We must do this if we would fulfill all of God's demands.'"

*Experience of God — experience of relatedness*

In such an experience we should expect to come to a deeper awareness and felt conviction about two things. We may not advert at the time to these realizations, any more than we are aware from day to day of the air we breathe, or of the growth of our bodies. But when we look back on our experience of God and our response to Him we should be able to see:

— First, that *God's identity as related to us* has become stronger, clearer to us. Jesus at the Jordan saw God descending upon Him as Spirit, heard God speaking to Him as Father. (And in this same Gospel scene we see Christ's own identity revealed as God the Son). In the beginning we may experience God in a pre-Christian way as Creator, Lawgiver and Judge. But as we ourselves mature and His grace within us ripens we experience God more and more in His true identity as Father, Son and Spirit.

— Secondly, *our own identity as related to God* is revealed more and more clearly to us, with deeper and stronger credibility. We hear the Father saying to us, in echo of His words to Jesus, "You are also my beloved son. My favor rests on you." We see Jesus presenting us to the Father with the words, "This is my Body; this is my own flesh and blood." We know that we are "in Christ" as members of His Body, acceptable to and loved by the Father as "sons in the Son." And the Spirit hovers over us with wide, protecting wings. We have a Paraclete, a Comforter, a Friend. He dwells within us as in a temple made holy by His presence (see *Ephesians* 2:20-22; 1 *Corinthians* 6:19).

Matthew follows his account of the preaching of John the Baptizer with the story of Christ's baptism in the Jordan. The first is a call to conversion; the second an experience of God. The connection between them is not just literary, but real: they go together.

When Paul was knocked to the ground by a light

from the sky and heard the voice of Jesus speaking to him, he was struck blind. Before he recovered his sight he had to ask, "Lord, what is it I must do?" It was in the act of his conversion that his experience of Jesus turned from blindness into light (see *Acts* 9:1 ff.; 22:6 ff.). Ever after, he knew that he had seen the Lord, and that he was called to be His apostle (see 1 *Corinthians* 15:8-10). When we accept Jesus it is also in an act (or many acts) of conversion. And this experience reveals to us who we are.

We may never have had a dramatic experience similar to St. Paul's. When we reflect back on our lives, however, we may realize that before we ever began to advert to the fact in any explicit way we were already and always aware of God relating to us as Father, Son and Spirit. And we were responding as His children, His Body, His temple. We may not have any conscious experience of "accepting Jesus" just because we have always accepted Him. But this doesn't make our acceptance — or our experience of Jesus — less real. Our acceptance and our experience of Jesus are as real as one thing: the choice we have made to believe that He is what He is for us and to base our lives on that belief.

This is why sins — especially sins rationalized or persevered in — block our experience of Jesus. In whatever measure we have "made our peace" with sin and accepted it as a part of our life, in that same measure we know — consciously or not — that we have not accepted Jesus. This is not true of the sins we fall into out of weakness, or because we are caught off guard. The sins we reject with our minds and hearts, struggle against, and are afflicted by do not have the effect of making Jesus a faraway reality to us. Our experience of abhorrence for these sins can be, in fact, an experience of relationship with Him. But the sins we love, the sins we make our own and feel possessive about, the sins we see as a chosen part of our life — these sins have the effect of drawing a curtain between us and the reality of Jesus Christ in our lives. Even though we say, and say sincerely, that we believe in Him; even though we continue to go to church; even though we may pray at times and do other things that are an expression of religion; still, if we are choosing to build into our life something that is incompatible with the teaching and desires of Jesus Christ for us, we know in our hearts that we are not building our lives on relationship with Him. No matter how much we rationalize or convince ourselves intellectually that our sins are not really sins, they will have the effect of numbing us to the experience of relationship with Christ.

For this reason, when people say that going to church is just "meaningless" to them; that Jesus Christ "doesn't seem real," or that Christianity just doesn't seem to "do anything" for them, the first (not the only) question they should ask themselves is whether they have already chosen to act in some ways that are incompatible with loyalty to Christ. We cannot expect the person of Jesus to have meaning for us in our hearts if we have already decided not to accept His words as having meaning for us for our lives.

The Gospel begins with a call to conversion. It is when we hear this call and respond to it that the heavens open to us. Then we are able to hear the Father's voice revealing to us the identity of Jesus and our own identity in words that apply to us both:

"This is my beloved Son. My favor rests on him."

## CHAPTER TWO: THE EXPERIENCE OF
## RELATEDNESS TO GOD — *Matthew* 3:13-17

*Summary:*

1. An experience of God does not have to be dramatic or emotional, or even identified in our consciousness with some one, particular moment.
2. We don't really know that our acceptance of Jesus is real until we experience ourselves taking Him for real. When we find ourselves living and acting in ways that simply do not make sense without faith, then we know that the gift of faith and of grace has been given us. The Spirit of Jesus is acting within us.
3. The most common experience of God consists in a series of very ordinary choices, spread out over a long period of time, which cannot be explained unless God is real to us; i.e., unless God has made Himself real to us, revealed Himself to us in a way that we take seriously.
4. We accept Jesus in an act (or many acts) of *choice* (conversion) in which we realize more clearly God's identity as related to us and our identity as related to Him.

*Questions for prayer and discussion:*

1. How have I experienced God in my life? Have I ever experienced His reality to me in the act of choosing to sin? Or was it after I had sinned? Have I experienced His reality to me in the act of choosing *not* to sin?
2. Have I experienced God's reality to me through prayer, or through the fact that I chose to pray? Through reading the Scriptures? Through the Sunday celebration? Through the use I have made of the sacraments? In these instances, did the experience of God depend on the amount of *faith* I brought to what I was doing? Did I have any other reason for taking part in these activities?
4. In what ways do I relate to each of the Three Persons of the Blessed Trinity? How do I relate to the Father as Father? To the Son as Savior and Teacher? To the Spirit as indwelling source of light, strength and love? How do I express these relationships in choices? How could I do this?

## CHAPTER THREE

## ACCEPTING THE LEVEL OF GOD

It may sound strange to say, but there are some sins which only our acceptance of Jesus makes us able to commit. We cannot be unfaithful to the word of God, for example, unless we have heard the word of God. We cannot sin against a covenant made with God until we have entered into a covenant with Him.

And we cannot be unfaithful to the mission of Jesus unless, as members of His Body on earth, we have received that mission as our own.

And so in his Gospel Matthew tells us about the temptations of Jesus — which are also our temptations — only after he has explained Christian conversion to us and the relationship with God to which it leads. The temptations he is dealing with here are not just ordinary temptations to do what is evil; they are temptations specifically against the divine level of relationship with God which is ours as Christians, which has been given to us with grace, and against the mission in this world to which we are called and consecrated by our identification with Christ. As disciples of Jesus we need to know what these temptations are.

As the Body of Christ on earth we — the Church — are called, like Christ, to be the saving presence of God among men. We are lifted up by baptism to share in God's life and nature, and consecrated to continue on earth Christ's triple mission as Prophet, Priest and King. But through the ages people always have been and always will be tempted to interpret the mission of Jesus — and that of the Church — in their own way and on their own level, according to their own human values and priorities. For this reason Matthew shows us Jesus confronting, in the very beginning of His public ministry, three temptations which His followers will have to be on guard against always. As "Master of the Way," Jesus is also the unmasker of deceit. He not only calls us to conversion and teaches us the true way of life. He also puts us on guard against the illusions which, under the appearance of good, would lure us into detours from that way.

By unmasking these temptations for us Matthew makes sure that our understanding is clear about the goal of Christ's mission and the means He makes use of to accomplish it. When we accept Jesus, we have to accept His mission to us for what it really is. And when we have committed ourselves to Him, His mission to us becomes in turn our mission to others.

Jesus' temptations in the desert follow immediately upon His baptism in the Jordan. It is logical that they should. Jesus has just seen the heavens opened and heard the Father's voice say, "This is my beloved Son." This experience may have been the event which finally brought His human mind to a clear, explicit realization that He Himself was the promised Messiah, the "Son of God."[1] If it was, we can understand why He needed to go apart and pray.

As we might expect, this was not an easy expe-

rience to absorb. Any one of us to whom God made
the revelation: "You are my chosen one; you are
destined to be the savior of the world" would want
time to think about it! It is not surprising that Jesus
felt the need to go apart by Himself and absorb in
faith what had been said to Him. Before He asked
anyone else to accept Him as savior of the world, He
had to accept Himself on this level, without any
watering-down of what that meant or called on Him
to be. This is what He went out into the desert to
wrestle with. Matthew tells us that the Spirit led Him
out into the wilderness to be alone, to pray. He
needed to reflect on His mission and to integrate into
His life all that the Father had told Him, all that He
had come to know about Himself and about what He
was sent to do.

The devil seizes the occasion. It must have been
hard for Jesus in His human nature, in His human
consciousness to grasp the fact that He was the
Messiah — just as it is hard for us to grasp the fact
that we are the Body of Christ and truly made divine,
truly sharers in the nature of God, by grace. The devil
suggests to Jesus ways of proving to Himself that He
really is the Son of God. "If you are the Son of God,"
he begins . . . words which will be echoed down the
ages under such forms as, "If the Church really is
what she claims to be . . . ," "If Christianity really is
the true religion . . . ," "If you say you are a religion of
love . . . " Jesus must maintain His faith in the
revelation of His own identity, while refusing to make
it credible to Himself or to others by adjusting His
mission to human expectations and desires.

The first temptation is to *change the goal* of
Christ's mission, and of the religion He taught, from
the transcendent goal of union with God to the

this-worldly goal of satisfying man's felt human needs on earth. This is a temptation which strikes at the heart of *faith,* substituting an obvious, human meaningfulness for the mystery of our call to share in the life of God.

"Command these stones to turn into bread," the devil says. The force of the temptation comes from the fact that Christ's followers do have as part of their mission on this earth the task of "turning stones into bread." The Christian meaning of work is to make nature serve man's needs, to change the wasteland of the world back into a graden of paradise in reversal of the curse of Adam's sin (see *Genesis* 2:15, 3:17-19). To provide bread for the hungry — out of the sweat of one's own brow — is a Christian value that converts the "curse" of work into a blessing.

This must always be a part of the mission of Christ's Church on earth: to work for a world of peace, justice and sufficiency for all men. But it must not be allowed to become the essential thrust of Christianity, for that would be to turn Christ's religion into nothing but a this-worldly idealism of purely humanitarian concerns. And explicit social reform was not part of Christ's own particular task on earth, any more than it was His task to extend the Church of God to the Gentiles. Those tasks would be taken up by His followers later, under the inspiration of the Holy Spirit (see, for example, *Matthew* 10:5-6; 15:24).

This mission of Jesus was to call us unambiguously beyond this world, beyond our felt human needs, to the satisfaction of our deepest (if unrecognized) hunger and thirst, which is for union with God in grace. Christ's religion is a summons, not to deny human life or human needs, but to transcend them.

There is something else offered to us that we hunger for even more: "Not on bread alone is man to live, but on every utterance that comes from the mouth of God."

Christ's mission, and the mission of the Church, must always be focused primarily on bringing people beyond what they already know, understand and feel a need for, to a hungry knowledge of God as revealed through His word, and to desire for total union of mind and heart and will with Him in grace. To let anything else be the ruling goal and focus of our ministry is to falsify the mission of Christ. It is also a most basic failure in faith. The "way" that Jesus is Master and teacher of is a way, not of human life alone, but of life on the level of God. To be His disciples means to lift up our thoughts and our desires to a whole new level of existence.

When we accept Jesus, then, we must accept Him knowing that He does not promise to satisfy all of our felt human needs on earth. He does not promise success or prosperity to His followers. He does not guarantee physical healing or even deliverance from mental anguish and emotional disturbances. Father Walter Ciszek, S.J., testified after spending twenty-three terrible years in Soviet prisons and labor camps: "I learned soon enough that prayer does not take away bodily pain or mental anguish. Nevertheless it does provide a certain moral strength to bear the burden patiently."[2]

Anyone who has read the account of Father Ciszek's experiences in *With God in Russia,* or the rest of his reflections on those experiences in *He Leadeth Me,* knows that prayer provided him, at least, with a great deal more than "a certain moral strength." It gave him sanctity — and the courage to endure in Russia with peace, courage and even joy. But it did not deliver him from his sufferings. It gave him courage to rise above them.

And this is what Jesus promises us: not the satisfaction of our felt human needs on the level on which we experience them, but the grace to rise above them, to transcend them; and to find a deeper, ultimate satisfaction in that which alone can satisfy our total human desire: union with God. "Our hearts were made for Thee, O God, and they shall not rest until they rest in Thee." St. Augustine said it in the name of us all.

The first temptation of Jesus was to offer us the bread we consciously hunger for instead of the bread that gives life. And yet the bread He gives is the true bread for which we hunger in the deepest core of our being: "Man does not live by bread alone, but by every word that comes from the mouth of God." Our real desire, whether we recognize it or not, is to know God and be united in love and in shared life with Him.

The question Jesus asks of all who would accept Him is, "Do you want what I came to give? Or would you too tempt me to change the stones into bread?"

*FOOTNOTES*

[1]We don't really know when, or in precisely what way, Jesus came to understand with His human intellect just who and what He was. As God and Second Person of the Blessed Trinity Jesus always knew exactly who He was. But there is no reason to suppose that His human intellect always shared, with explicit and conscious clarity, in this knowledge. Like the rest of us, Jesus had to *grow into* an understanding of His own unique meaning and value to God. He had to learn the "name" and the mission the Father had given Him. The same is true of each one of us. (For further development of this, see Jacques Guillet, S.J., *The Consciousness of Jesus,* tr. Edmond Bonin, Newman Press, 1972, especially pp. 43-46). See also *Choosing Life* by John

English, S.J. (Paulist Press, 1978), for the way we come to realize our own identity before God.

[2]*He Leadeth Me,* by Walter J. Ciszek, S.J., Image Books, 1975, p. 64. See also *With God in Russia,* same authors and publishers.

## CHAPTER THREE: ACCEPTING THE LEVEL OF GOD — *Matthew* 4:1-4

*Summary:*

1. The devil tempted Jesus to prove His identity by changing stones into bread — that is, by using His power to satisfy man's felt human needs in this world.
2. By resisting this temptation Jesus showed that the goal of His religion is not just humanitarianism or the good life in this world, although this is the proper goal of politics and of Christian social action.
3. He taught instead that His mission was to satisfy the desire of man's heart for that relationship with God which only God can give. In this way He calls us to faith in the transcendent destiny offered to man with grace. "Not by bread alone is man to live, but on every utterance that comes from the mouth of God."

*Questions for prayer and reflection:*

1. What needs do I look to my religion to satisfy? What do I ask God for most frequently in prayer? What help do I seek from my pastor? What is the last thing I asked him to do for me? What need did this fulfill?
2. How often do I turn to the word of God for personal nourishment? How much of the Scriptures have I read? How much time do I give to reflection on the word of God? Have I ever asked anyone to teach me to pray over the Scriptures? To pray with me?
3. What is there in my life that would show or demonstrate unambiguously my own belief that man is not to live by bread alone? Do I ever leave any of my felt human needs unsatisfied in order to take time for prayer?

## CHAPTER FOUR

## THE ACCEPTANCE OF ABSOLUTE TRUST

The second illusion Jesus unmasks for us as "Master of the Way" is the temptation to *change the means* God chose for the establishment of His Kingdom. Out in the desert Jesus is urged by the devil (as we all are) to place His confidence, not in God's way of saving the world, but in other means which seem more reasonable or more effective to our natural, human way of looking at things.

The devil takes Jesus to the top of the Temple, and invites Him to throw Himself down into the courtyard below, in the midst of all the people. After all, Jesus risks nothing. If He really is the Son of God, the Father will keep Him from harm. It would even be an act of faith in Scripture, which says, "He will bid his angels take care of you" (see Psalm 91).

At its core this is a temptation to base one's trust in God, not on the fact of who God is, or on His loving fidelity to His covenant, or on the promise of His word but on the visible signs and wonders He accomplishes.

Jesus is being asked by God to believe He is the Messiah, the chosen Savior of the world. The devil tempts Him to insist on visible signs and wonders as proof of God's presence, of God's power, of God's protection. If Jesus is to undertake God's work with confidence, God must show Him that He intends to work with Him, to accompany Him, to make His efforts successful. For Jesus to believe that He is indeed the chosen, the Anointed One, God must give proof of His favor. And this proof takes the form of physical protection; that is what Psalm 91 is all about.

We who have read the end of the story know that the passion and death of Jesus — His deliverance into the hands of His enemies — was in Jewish eyes the point-by-point contradiction of everything Psalm 91 expresses. According to the interpretation of this Psalm, as it was understood in Christ's time, when God abandoned Jesus to His persecutors, He clearly showed that Jesus did *not* enjoy God's favor, that He was *not* the Anointed One, not the Messiah. Obviously Jesus did not "dwell in the shelter of the Most High" and could not say to the Lord "My refuge and my fortress, my God in whom I trust." Obviously the Lord had not given command to His angels about Jesus to bear Him up, lest He dash His foot against a stone, because Jesus was in fact lifted up on the cross and cast down into the grave.

Psalm 91 says of the just man, the one who enjoys God's favor, "Because he clings to me, I will deliver him . . . He shall call upon me, and I will answer him; I will be with him in distress." If this was true of the just man in general, it was even more true of God's specially chosen one, the Messiah. When the Jews taunted Jesus beneath the cross, saying, "He saved others but he cannot save himself! So he is the king of Israel! Let's see him come down from that cross and then we will believe in him," this was the significance of their words. They were holding up against Jesus the promise of Psalm 91 and of other passages in Scripture that are like it, and saying, "This proves you are not the Messiah; you are deluded and an imposter." The jeering words under the cross: "He relied on God; let God rescue him now if he wants to. After all, he claimed, 'I am God's Son'" (see *Matthew* 27:39-44) simply expressed the prevailing theological attitude behind the sentence already passed on Jesus during His trial: "He has blasphemed!" (see *Matthew* 26:65). The Messiah ("God's Son") would not be handed over to His enemies. God would not allow it. But God did allow Jesus to be handed over. Therefore His claim to be the Anointed Son of God was false. And to insist on this claim even after it was obvious God was not protecting Him was blasphemy.[1]

Accepting Jesus means accepting to trust absolutely in God — in His love, in His presence, in His power, in His protection, in His favor and help — without insisting on any visible signs or proof that He is with us. This is trust based on nothing but who God is in Himself — on His love and fidelity — and on the promise of His word. It is the trust Jesus modelled for us during His temptations in the desert and in the depths of His abandonment on the cross. To those who are still weak in faith (as which one of us isn't?) God may show signs and proof of His favor by granting prosperity, success, popularity, or even the power to work miracles! But as soon as we rely on these signs and wonders, or insist on them as a condition for believing that we are loved and chosen by God, we have succumbed to the second temptation Jesus faced in the desert. From that moment on our acceptance of Jesus is flawed and falsified at the roots.

There is another side to this temptation. Jesus

was not only tempted to insist on signs and wonders as a condition for His own belief in His call: He was also tempted to perform them in order to win credibility from others. The devil did not tempt Jesus to throw Himself down from just any precipice, as a way of finding out for Himself alone whether the Father would support Him. Matthew says the devil took Him to the pinnacle of the Temple and urged Him to throw Himself down from there. The temptation here was for Jesus to win credibility for Himself by an impressive sign, a miracle. It was the temptation to "Madison Avenue" evangelization. The Temple was the center of Jerusalem's life and activity. To jump off the Temple was like jumping off a skyscraper into the middle of Times Square. If Jesus came floating down from the Temple into the bustling middle of Jerusalem the whole town would be impressed. They would certainly find it easier to accept His claim that He was sent from God if He introduced Himself this way than they would if He came to them on ground level, poor and without contacts, out of the country village of Nazareth.

The devil's basic argument here is a slogan well known in the business and advertising world: "Nothing succeeds like success." If Jesus wants to win followers, He should show that He is a winner.

Jesus answers by recalling the way His people "put God to the test" in the desert (see *Exodus* 17:1-7) by insisting that He provide for their needs not in His own way and in His own time, but by conforming His acts of power to the clamor of their own emotions and fears. They issued an "ultimatum" to God by making His immediate response to their prayer a *condition* for their continued faith and trust in Him. Jesus makes clear that to be His followers we must trust in

Him, as He does in the Father, unconditionally, no matter how obvious it might seem to us at times that God has abandoned us. And we must insist that others trust Him in the same way. Like Jesus Himself we must establish the Kingdom by the means the Father has chosen and not depart from these regardless of any apparent consequences to ourselves or to our mission. Even if we are delivered up to failure and death we must be faithful to His way and trust in God for the outcome.

Christ's Kingdom is founded on those means that help us to rely on God: on weakness and humility; on love and trust in the Father. It is not established by reliance on human means: on wealth, power or prestige (see 2 *Corinthians* 12:5-10). It is essentially the work of God, not of man; and we can be instrumental in establishing the Kingdom only to the extent that we are united to God in faith, hope and obedient love. We must place absolute trust in the power of God to accomplish His purposes through any means He chooses. "For God's folly is wiser than men, and his weakness more powerful than men" (1 *Corinthians* 1:25). To assume that God's ways and man's ways are the same in the work of divine salvation is to operate out of a basic misunderstanding between ourselves and Jesus Christ. It is to put our acceptance of Jesus on a false basis.

Jesus will not cast Himself down from the Temple, because the only motivation He could have for this would be to impress Himself or others with His ability to command the power of God. That is not a motivation He will act out of. When Jesus calls upon His divine power it is to save, not to impress. The motive is compassion, not public relations. And as "Master of the Way" He teaches us to do the same.

Above all, Jesus teaches us in His response to this temptation to trust absolutely in the compassion and providence of God. We must adhere to God in hope, regardless of how unintelligible His ways may appear to us to be in our times of darkness, abandonment and distress. God's ways are not our ways. If we are to follow Jesus as "Master of the Way" it must be with a faith and a hope that depend, not on visible results, but simply on our knowledge of who God is. This is the only trust in God that is properly divine. And this is the trust Christ teaches to all who would accept and follow Him as disciples along His way.

### FOOTNOTE

[1]See the explanation of this argument in my previous book: *Questions For Today: WHY JESUS?* chapter eleven "Jesus Is Victory" (Dimension Books, 1981).

### CHAPTER FOUR: THE ACCEPTANCE OF ABSOLUTE TRUST — *Matthew* 4:5-7

*Summary:*

1. The devil tempted Jesus to justify His own trust in God and to win credibility from others by "forcing" God to work an impressive miracle. This is a temptation to base one's own trust on signs and wonders and to establish the Kingdom by catering to the prejudices and assumptions of men.
2. Jesus knew that the Kingdom consists in a total surrender of man to God in faith, hope and love. It is established by God's power, not man's. And therefore the means to establish the Kingdom are those which show our absolute surrender to God in faith, dependence on God in hope, obedience to God in love.
3. By resisting this temptation Jesus teaches us to trust absolutely in God's way and to follow it without doubting or yielding to human fears and assumptions. To insist that God do things our way is to "put God to the test."

*Questions for prayer and discussion:*

1. On what do I base my belief that God loves me, has chosen me, protects me and is working with me? Does my trust in God's favor toward me go up and down according to the signs I see that He is blessing me? What true and solid reasons do I have for believing in God's love and care for me?

2. What means do I think the Church should use to fulfill her mission? Are these the means most visible in the activity and pastoral work of my parish? Have I ever supported a policy in my church that catered to human prejudices?

3. What means do I myself use to accomplish my purposes in my family and social life? In my business and civic life? Are any of these means contrary to the values and priorities taught by Jesus? How much do I actively trust in God in these areas of my life?

*CHAPTER FIVE*

*A COMMITMENT TO UNDIVIDED LOVE*

As "Master of the Way," what Jesus teaches us above all is how to love. To accept Him as Teacher is to accept Him as a teacher of love. The greatest temptation against love, however, is love itself. Once people have begun to love in any measure — love the world, love other people, love God — the love they have can be used as a lever to pry them off of their adherence to love that is authentic, total and pure. And this is what Christ's response to His third temptation teaches us: how to love God with an undivided heart.

The third temptation of Christ is a temptation to be unfaithful to God out of love for God; or at least out of love for God's Kingdom. It is at one and the same time the most straightforward and the most deceitful of all the temptations of Jesus. And no one is subject to it in its full force and subtlety except those who have learned to love.

The devil took Jesus up "a very high mountain and displayed before him all the kingdoms of the world in their magnificence" *(Matthew* 4:8). He then said to Jesus: "I will give you all this power and the glory of these kingdoms; the power has been given to me and I give it to whomever I wish. Prostrate yourself in homage before me, and it shall all be yours" *(Luke* 4:6-7).

This is a straight deal. In the first two temptations the devil was being deceitful. He was quoting Scripture in a false but believable sense, trying to make falsehood appear as truth and the lesser good appear as the greater. But in the third temptation he is being honest. He is saying, "I will help you achieve the very real and tangible good that you desire — any world order of peace and justice, any economic arrangement, any cultural environment of right attitudes, values and behavior; any 'kingdom of heaven' that you desire to establish on earth — if in return you will do one thing for me: acknowledge rightness in me alongside the rightness of God." All Jesus has to do is accept that under certain circumstances evil can be good — or that evil means can be justified for the sake of a good enough end — and the devil will put at His disposal for the establishment of the Kingdom all of the power and wealth that he controls.

It is an honest offer. The fact is — to all appearances, at least — the devil does control an enormous percentage of the power and wealth of this world. If that statement sounds extreme or even mythological, then let us just say that, by and large, most of the power and wealth of the world do not seem to be put at the service of even authentically human values, let alone the values of the Gospel. In our world an enormous percentage of most national budgets is devoted to making devilish instruments of war. Even if in some countries this is a necessity, made so by the sinful aggression of others, as many people believe it is, still it is money spent on the devil's game. And no proportionate amount is being spent to eliminate the injustices and oppression which are causes of war throughout the world.

Another example is the media industry. The very fact that the performing arts are now looked upon as an "industry" gives the whole game away: the growing goal of movie and television productions is neither "art for art's sake" nor art for the sake of benefiting humanity in any way. What determines the content of the shows is not "the good, the true and the beautiful" but the ratings. Shows are produced to make money, and those who produce them are guided more and more by what will sell. The immeasurable power of the media industry is put at the service of money, and those who have the money wield the power of tube and screen in every neighborhood and home.

This same analysis could be applied to business after business, industry after industry. In the measure that profit as such becomes the ruling goal of a business, that business is falling away from the service of humanity as its primary reason for existing. We can be grateful that not all businesses are ruled by profit motivation alone. But in whatever measure a business makes profit its practical god, the devil can say of that business, "It's power has been given to me."

In this temptation the devil offers to put at Christ's service all the influence he exerts through playing on men's desire for power and wealth. He will move people to use all their resources to help establish any social order, religion, cultural reforms, government or society Jesus asks. And this is a deal that is meant sincerely. It is a straightforward trade-off, with no deception behind it.

At the same time, it is the most deceitful of all the temptations. This is not because the devil is engaging in trickery. It is because the temptation to idolatry is by its very nature the most subtle and seductive temptation human beings are subject to. And idolatry is what this temptation is all about.

"Idolatry" to us means "worshipping idols." We think of uncultured savages bowing down before grotesque sculptures and assuaging their god's thirst for blood with superstitious sacrifices. Idolatry to us means something primitive, unenlightened and naive.

In reality idolatry just means letting any value that is less than God determine the direction of our lives. Culture is a breeder, not a dispeller of idols. When we have such a deep appreciation for any human value that in practice we let it become the ultimate focus of our energies — or at least of a major percentage of our energies — then we have fallen into idolatry.

Art is an idol for some people. They have such a keen sense of beauty that they devote their lives to bringing it into existence, with no thought beyond the goodness of beauty as such.

"Beauty is truth, truth beauty," — that is all
Ye know on earth and all ye need to know.

*(Ode on a Grecian Urn)*

When John Keats wrote these lines he was simply giving eloquent, masterful expression to his idolatry.

For others war is the supreme, practical value of their lives. In the movie "Patton" we have a stereotype (historians will say whether it is fictional or real) of the kind of mind which invented Mars, the god of war. The man presented to us as General George S. Patton in that movie lived for the thrill and power of combat. Had he been a Roman general in the centuries before Christ instead of an American of our times, he would have offered incense before some statue designed to make visible, or at least to artistically suggest, the beauty and the glory of *homo bellicosus,* of Martial Man.

We Americans do not consciously erect statues to our gods. But without knowing it, we do exactly what the ancient Greeks and Romans did: we inevitably and spontaneously, because we are human beings, pay homage in graphic, pictorial form to the values our society is most conscious of. Our city streets are lined with images of Venus. Billboard after billboard proclaims our nation's devotion to sex. Our public rituals pay homage to the same goddess. Young girls are sought out whose bodies are capable of presenting in most enticing form the attractions of sexual delight, and they compete for the honor of appearing at parades and games and festivals dressed as maids and priestesses of the cult.

For those who know how to read them, our society abounds in status symbols which identify the devotees of the god Mammon. Devotion to Vulcan, the god of technology, is evident everywhere. And the goddess of fertility is worshipped by our society as she has never been by any society before us: not, in our times, for the sake of increasing the birthrate, but for the sake of controlling it. Each year over a million babies in the United States alone are sacrifice, in the cold, silent ritual of abortion to the goddess of planned population.[1]

This is idolatry. It is, in everything except the name we give to it, indistinguishable from the worship that pagan civilizations gave to their gods and goddesses. Those deities were nothing but symbols and personifications of the various values a particular society identified as its own. The pagan rituals we look down on with such superiority were in reality a more conscious, sophisticated celebration of values than the unwitting liturgies of sex and power and fertility control that we engage in. At least the pagans knew what they were doing.

The thing we have to keep in mind is that in almost every case idolatry is the worship of something good. The values can easily be distorted, of course, even in the celebration of them. Idolatry can degenerate, as so much of it has in our country, into grossness and human sacrifice. But idolatry as such presupposes the recognition of real human values. It takes an appreciative person to be a devout idolator. And this is what makes idolatry so deceptive. Authentic devotion to any false god, be it money, sex, power, fertility control, technology, or even to revelry (represented by Bacchus) has as its core of truth and goodness the recognition and appreciation of some real human value.

What makes idolatry evil is not appreciation of the human value, but non-appreciation of the transcendent value of God. The only reason *not* to put our lives at the service of some authentic human value is the realization that we are called to put them at the service of the uncreated God. And therefore anyone who does not know God, and who at the same time is not an idolator, should look into his appreciation of human values. Harsh as it sounds to say it, he may be just a swine.

Idolatry, of course, is not exclusive. A monotheistic idolator is almost a contradiction in terms. No human value contains within itself the goodness of all the rest. And therefore idolators tend to pay homage to many gods, balancing off against one another the values of money, power, sexual love, fertility, revelry, etc. One or the other goal (value, god) may be the dominant one — a particular person's life may be, and usually is, ruled by some predominant appreciation and drive — but no one value can claim the idolator's total and exclusive devotion. No matter what one's principal god may be, there are always other gods alongside him.

Now we see the mind-shattering impact of the First Commandment on human thinking. When God thundered from Sinai: "I, the LORD, am your God ... You shall not have other gods besides me," He was striking at the very core of idolatry. The idolator recognizes many values as worth living for; he uses now one, now another to determine the direction and orientation of his life. But the idolator accepts no value, no reality as being great enough to claim anyone's exclusive devotion. The respect given to one value must be tempered by the respect that is owed to others. Uprightness is a matter of maintaining a just balance.

And so what we in our civilization call "religion," or the worship of God as such, is a definite value to the idolator. But so is making money, having friends, helping the poor, reforming society, enjoying life, and being loyal to those one loves. To the idolator, the idea of paying homage to God alone, with no other life-directing values besides Him, is an abomination. It is narrowness, fanaticism, a denial of obvious good.

In other words, it is one thing to acknowledge that God is God, and the greatest of all values. It is quite another thing to say that there are no other gods — no other life-directing values — besides Him. Yet this is what the First Commandment calls upon us to do. And it is re-emphasized in the formula which became the watchword of God's People:

> Hear, O Israel! The LORD is our God, the LORD
> alone! Therefore, you shall love the LORD, your
> God, with *all* your heart, and with *all* your soul, and
> with *all* your strength. *(Deuteronomy* 6:4-5; emphasis
> added)

This formula is in no way a denial of human
values. The person who lives by it will not be callous
to the poor, to family loyalties, to the needs of
humankind. The First Commandment is not directed
downward, against appreciation of any human value,
but upward, to the recognition of the all-transcending
value of God. The meaning of this Commandment is
simply that God is not one value among others. There
is no just balance of fidelity to maintain between
Himself and them. God is All, and nothing else is
anything except through reference to Him. When
Christians seek to reform society, to help the poor, to
make a living for themselves and to love one another,
they see these activities as having their real value from
the fact they are ways of serving God. Any one of
these activities carried to a point of opposition to
God's will, would lose its meaning and value.

This is why any human value, no matter how
true, how sacred or how real, given a place, not just
above, but even alongside of God, becomes an idol.
Now that the Lord has revealed Himself to us and we
know Him for what He is, there can be for us no other
gods, no other life-directing values alongside of Him.
He is All. And every other value that we seek or pay
homage to, we must look for, not alongside of God,
but in Him. All true values, all true good is found in
God — within the embrace of His will, His teaching,

His service. Nothing that is good can be in competition with Him.

The third temptation of Jesus is not a temptation to anything evil directly. Its direct focus is on nothing but what is good: the enhancement of human life on earth through the promotion of real values; in fact, through the establishment of the Kingdom. But this is with the understanding that obedience to God is not an absolute value. The Kingdom the devil proposes is a divided Kingdom. It is characterized by fragmented loyalty to God and to lesser values. And this is, in reality, the most subtle of all evils: it is the fall into idolatry.

This is above all the temptation of the generous. Those who are able to burn with zeal for justice; to love another person with all-sacrificing devotion; to dedicate themselves to a cause — these are the ones to whom the devil whispers, "All this will I give you, if only you will accord me a place — the smallest of all places — alongside your allegiance to God." Thus terrorists resort to violence for the sake of social reform; businessmen justify dishonesty for the good of supporting their families; lovers continue in adultery for fear of causing pain to one another; and all of us, on the day-to-day level of our ordinary living, excuse impatience and violence toward others as the "only way to get things done," or to "get our point across."

This third temptation of Jesus is forthright. It is a naked matching of the immediate, obvious, created good against the remote, intangible and abstract-sounding good of "God's will." It is the ultimate test of faith, hope and love. There is no deceptiveness about this temptation except that which comes from our human inability to grasp the transcendent greatness of God. The only lie in it is the spontaneous prejudice of our minds which inclines us to believe that good can still be good even when chosen against the will of God. Jesus will confront this temptation again — many times, in fact — until He overcomes it for the last time by letting go of life itself on the cross.

To the devil's proposal in the desert Jesus offers no argument. To argue about ultimate loyalty to God is already to lose. As "Master of the Way" He responds to this temptation with a simple reaffirmation of the rock-bottom reality, the fundamental principle and first rule of all human action on earth: "You shall do homage to the Lord your God; him alone shall you adore."

This is the absolute love for God which frees us to be authentic in all our other loves. When we accept Jesus Christ we accept to love God absolutely and everything else only in relationship to Him. Since everything else *exists* only through its relationship to God, this is the only love which is true to the reality of created people and things. Acceptance of Jesus, then, is a commitment to love God and all else that exists with an unfragmented heart.

*FOOTNOTE*

[1]James Michener's historical novel *The Source* brings out in graphic, if fictional, detail how fertility rites and child sacrifice are logically connected. Nations whose highest value is human life are willing to sacrifice individual human lives to preserve the life of the whole — or even to maintain that quality of life to which the nation has grown accustomed. See *The Source,* "Level XIV: Death and Life" (Random House, 1965).

## CHAPTER FIVE: A COMMITMENT TO
## UNDIVIDED LOVE — *Matthew* 4:8-11

*Summary:*

1. The devil offers to help Jesus with all of the human wealth and power he controls to establish any religion or reforms in the social order that Jesus desires if only Jesus will put the *work to be accomplished* ahead of the will of God. To do this is to deny the infinite transcendence of God's being and goodness, and to give the devil a place alongside of God.

2. Jesus answers with an echo of the First Commandment which is the heart and soul of Judaism (see *Deuteronomy* 6:4-5; "Hear, O Israel . . . "). God is not one god among many; His will is not one value to be respected among many values. Apart from the will of God there is no good. Therefore for no reason, cause, or apparent good to be achieved should man in any way go against the will of God. To let any value less than God Himself determine the direction of our lives is idolatry.

3. Jesus teaches us here that we must accept to love God as our total good — that is, supremely, single-heartedly, without conditions — or we are not loving Him authentically as God. We cannot love God as our All with hearts that are divided between Him and something else. (Cf. *Matthew* 5:33 and 22:36-38).

*Questions for prayer and discussion:*

1. Can I think of any person or group who in my opinion has accepted to do evil for the sake of accomplishing good? Have I ever been tempted to this myself? Can I appreciate and sympathize with the strength of this temptation?

2. What values, persons or causes mean so much to me that they determine the direction of my life? Could I be tempted to sin for their sake? How could I love these realities "in" God instead of alongside of God? What does it mean to say that God is All Good and that outside of relationship to Him there can be no true good?

3. What can I do to work toward loving God with my whole heart, my whole mind and my whole strength? Do I really believe that if I seek first the kingship of God over me, His way of holiness, then everything else I need will be provided for me? And for those I love?

# CHAPTER SIX

## ACCEPTING PRAYER
## AS A NORMAL PART OF LIFE

As disciples of Jesus we are called to follow a way of life which is at one and the same time the fulfillment of all our human capacity and desires, and yet utterly beyond our human abilities and even our natural, human understanding of values. This is why Jesus told us, "Avoid being called teachers. Only one is your teacher, the Messiah" *(Matthew* 23:10). The way that Jesus is Master of is not a way of human wisdom, one that any human being can ever totally master. It is the way of thinking, of living and of loving that is unique to God Himself. And only God can teach it.

This is why Christian discipleship is essentially a life of prayer.

By a "life of prayer" we don't mean, of course, a life given over exclusively, or even primarily, to solitude and meditation. A "life of prayer" is a life whose basic direction comes from personal communication with God. Prayer is nothing but personal communication with God. This can take many forms. But when this personal communication with God becomes the guidance system of one's life, one is living a "life of prayer." And until it does, one is not fully a disciple of Jesus Christ.

To accept Jesus, then, means to accept prayer as an integral part of one's life. And this prayer is designed to be a guidance system. It is the prayer of discipleship.

The word "disciple" just means "student." It is unfortunate that as the word came to be used more and more in an exclusively religious sense we lost sight of its original meaning. We often think that "disciple" of Jesus is synonymous with "Christian" or "follower" of Jesus. But this is not what the word means. The word means "student," and anyone who is not actually engaged — in some way or another: through significant listening, reading, or deep, personal reflection — in "studying" the mind and heart of Christ is not actually a disciple.

In the beginning, and to some extent all of our lives, we learn about Jesus from others. But discipleship is only authentic in the measure that Jesus is teaching us Himself. "Only one is your teacher, the Messiah." And "No one knows the Son but the Father, and no one knows the Father but the Son — and anyone to whom the Son wishes to reveal him" *(Matthew* 11:27). Even if the medium of Christ's communication with us is the preaching or teaching of human beings — whether through formal instructions, spiritual books or personal conversation — it is still the direct action of Jesus on our hearts, the enlightening, motivating power of His Spirit, which makes our learning and our response discipleship.

Discipleship, then, whatever outward form it takes, must always include an essential core of deep, personal reflection on God's Self-revelation to us which leads to a response of heart and will. For this reason discipleship is ultimately individual: we have to learn from Jesus ourselves. Each one of us has to. We learn in the *context* of an ecclesial faith-community, and we do not presume to set up our own experience of God against the ages-old, common experience of the Church. We are disciples *in* the Church, and disciples *of* the Jesus who teaches through His Church. But to be disciples at all we have to learn from Christ ourselves, personally and individually. And this means to learn through deep, reflective prayer as well as through everything else.

Accordingly, before Matthew shows us Jesus actually beginning to teach (which He does for the first time in Matthew's Gospel in the Sermon on the Mount), he first shows us Jesus doing what every disciple of His must do in order to learn from Him: he shows us Jesus going apart by Himself to pray.

Right after the temptations in the desert Matthew tells us that Jesus "withdrew to Galilee." This was to fulfill Isaiah's prophecy:

> "Land of Zebulun, and of Naphtali
> along the sea beyond the Jordan,
> heathen Galilee:
> a people living in darkness
> has seen a great light.
> On those who inhabit a land
> overshadowed by death,
> light has arisen."

> *(Matthew* 4:12, 15-16)

Two words give us the key to this passage. They are "withdrew" and "light."

The Greek word translated here as "withdrew": *anachoreo* (from which our English word "anchorite" — hermit — comes), is used four times of Jesus in

Matthew's Gospel. Each time it is in a context of withdrawing from conflict or opposition (see *Matthew* 4:12; 12:15; 14:14; 15:21). The same word is used of Jesus twice by Mark and John and in the same context (see *Mark* 3:7; *John* 6:15). In most cases it is clear that the withdrawing is for the sake of greater aloneness and solitude. (See also the kindred word: *hypochoreo,* in *Luke* 5:16 and 9:10).

The lesson is clear enough. As "Master of the Way" Jesus is teaching us by example that the way to come into the light is to withdraw — for a time, at least — from the darkness. When we experience the turmoil and confusion that arise within us because of emotions, passions, appetites, compulsions or prejudices, the response to this is to go apart and pray. It doesn't matter whether the opposition comes from within ourselves or from others; once we find ourselves in a state of conflict or confusion about the way we should live out the Gospel, our first step when possible should be to "withdraw."

This withdrawal is for the sake of clearer communication with God. We withdraw to be with Jesus. For this reason we distance ourselves from anything that clouds the issue or causes darkness within us. We also go apart, insofar as we can, from whatever distracts us from prayer — at least for those moments which we are able to give exclusively to reflection and prayer as such.

The withdrawal we are talking about is not exactly the same thing as getting away by ourselves to think. Sometimes just going off to think can be a step into deeper darkness: we just deliver ourselves over to all the emotions, fears, anger, desires and one-sided scripts that may be running through our minds. What many of us call "prayer" is just time spent in solitary

— and usually ineffective — problem-solving. We go away to brood over our problems. The fact that we may brood on our knees or in church — or even in a complaining monologue with God — does not suffice to turn this into prayer.

It does happen, of course, that sometimes we can take our problems to God and find solutions. It is not excluded that such an exercise might be authentic prayer. But it frequently isn't. And the best way to insure that this kind of problem-solving will be prayer when one has to engage in it is to begin the session by listening to Jesus instead of asking Him to listen to us. This means that we begin by looking, not at our problem or for its solution, but at something Jesus said or did, just for the sake of understanding it — for the sake of entering into His mind, His viewpoint, His desires. Instead of looking at our problem and trying to direct the light of Christ upon it, we simply go into the light of Christ for its own sake and let it shine on our lives where it will. Quite frequently we will find it illuminating just that area which has been keeping our problem in its darkness.

The light we seek through times of Christian withdrawal is Christ. It is not just a matter of quieting our souls so that the light that is within us — some deep, subconscious perception of truth that is already ours — might emerge. There are times when such an exercise is quite effective; when all we really need to do is get in touch with ourselves, with our own "gut" feelings, in order to know what we want or believe we ought to do. But Christian withdrawal involves more than that. It is not simply a technique for achieving inner stillness. The light we seek is not some deeper level of our own consciousness, but that divine and saving light which belongs to Christ alone. It is to "a people living in darkness" that He comes with His new light, and "to those who inhabit a land overshadowed by death."

When it comes to thinking about the things of God, the starting point of our minds, conditioned as we are by our culture and inclined as we are to sin, is darkness. We live in the deadening shadow of sin, in a cultural environment of attitudes and values which reflect our own sins and the sins of others down the ages. The light we need to live by is a saving, redeeming light. It is a light which comes from "outside" of us in the sense that it is Christ's light, not ours. And yet it is within us through the life of grace and the Holy Spirit who has been poured out in our hearts. It is a light which is both interior and "other" to us at the same time.

The withdrawal Jesus teaches, therefore, is a positive effort to communicate with the living, personal God. This God has revealed Himself in Jesus Christ and He continues to reveal Himself — as He chooses, and freely — to those who seek Him.

No technique enables us to achieve Christian enlightenment, because it is a free gift. The light that enlightens us is a personal communication from God's mind to our own. But since God has chosen, through Jesus, to communicate with us in human words — in the intelligible speech of our own daily language — we are able to enter into communication with His mind and heart simply by taking His words seriously. This involves using our human faculties of memory, intellect and will to recall or re-read what Jesus said; to ask questions about the meaning of His words or gestures, and try to answer them; and to take a stance with our wills toward what we come to understand; that is, to respond with decisions and choices.[1]

As we engage in this process, God assists us from within, of course, by the light and power of His Spirit. If He did not, then Christ's words — no matter how intelligible they are in themselves — would simply leave us inert. They would have no more practical effect on us than poetry on a pig!

To be a disciple means to let oneself be taught. And this means we accept the teaching method of the Master. The method of Jesus was to address our thinking minds with intelligible words, and to live out visibly in His own human actions the truth and the values He came to reveal. And so it is by using our minds to reflect on His words and by using our imaginations to contemplate His actions on earth that we enter into the school of Jesus as His disciples. This method may lack the thrill of the mysterious and esoteric; it may seem too ordinary and too human to promise great results. But it is the method Jesus chose to employ as "Master of the Way"; and it is the first method which the saints and mystics of Christianity recommend to those would would be His disciples.[2]

Later, if we persevere in discipleship, the method may very well change. We may find ourselves unable to pray any longer by reasoning and reflecting on the Scriptures. When this happens, it may be the signal that it is time for us to pass from meditation on the word of God to a more simple form of contemplation; to prayer that has less and less to do with words or images. Normally this moment comes only after one has spent considerable time reflecting with one's intellect on God's word, pondering it deeply, and trying to live by it purely in practice. We have the testimony of St. John of the Cross on this, as well as that of the author of *The Cloud of Unknowing*. As the author of *The Cloud* puts it: "I want you to understand clearly that for beginners and those a little advanced in contemplation, reading or hearing the word of God must precede pondering it, and without time given to serious reflection there will be no genuine prayer."[3]

As "Master of the Way," then, Jesus teaches us that it is only by the light of prayer that we can see to follow the way along which He would lead us. His own "withdrawal" in the face of conflict and opposition is an example to us. This withdrawal is neither flight from the world nor a refusal to meet the challenge of life in this world. It is simply an entering into the light of God in order to see how the challenge should best be confronted.

The fact that this "withdrawal" of Christ's takes place immediately before He begins His public mission of preaching and teaching (see *Matthew* 4:17) is of special significance, perhaps. It suggests that before we will really be able to choose a life work — or direct the work we have already chosen to the establishment of God's Kingship on earth — we need to "go aside" in some significant way with Christ in prayer.

Few people are able to "withdraw" from the life and activity of this world in a physical way. It is not the custom in western civilization, as it is in some of the eastern countries, for people to spend six months or a year in a monastery in order to find direction for their lives. But some form of prayerful withdrawal from the pace and conditioning of our culture would seem to be both possible and desirable.[4]

When we "go apart" with Christ we allow both our minds and our affections, our thoughts and our desires, to find their true center. By freeing ourselves from the artificial pressures of life in our society we enable the inclinations of our hearts — our graced inclinations — to make themselves felt. We remain free to follow these inclinations or not, but at least we have a clearer idea of what we are drawn to and by what or whom.

Christian discipleship, then, calls for times of withdrawal: a few moments of "quiet time" in the day; a "sabbath hour" perhaps, on certain days; a "hermit day" *(poustinia)*⁵ once in a while; a weekend of retreat or spiritual input when the occasion presents itself. Any time spent in spiritual reading — of the Scriptures or other books — is an exercise of Christian withdrawal and discipleship. So is the affective withdrawal of our desires from anything that competes with perfect purity of heart. And when we give ourselves to this kind of withdrawal with and for Christ the prophecy comes true for us:

A people living in darkness
has seen a great light.
On those who inhabit a land
overshadowed by death,
light has arisen.

When Jesus, the "Master of the Way," calls us apart, He reveals Himself to us as the Light of the world. To fully accept Him as the Light that He is, we need to build into our lives moments of withdrawal from the darkness, when, in response to His invitation, we go apart with Him and let His words illuminate our minds. This is what it means to become His disciples and to accept Him as "Master of the Way."

### FOOTNOTES

¹For a developed explanation of this way of praying, which is the classical Christian method of "meditation" or mental prayer, see my book *His Way,* chapters 3 and 4 (St. Anthony Messenger Press, 1977).

[2]See, for example, *The Autobiography of St. Teresa of Avila,* chapter 22; St. Ignatius of Loyola, *The Spiritual Exercises,* paragraphs 45-54; 73-81; 101-109; 130; and 238-260; St. Francis de Sales, *Introduction to the Devout Life,* Part II.

[3]See John of the Cross, *Ascent of Mount Carmel,* Book II, ch. 13 for the three signs that indicate it is time to pass from the active methods of meditation and contemplation to more simple contemplation. See *The Cloud of Unknowing,* ch. 35, on the necessity of reading, thinking and prayer for the contemplative. This corresponds to the old monastic formula: *lectio, reflectio, contemplatio.* (I have quoted from the Image Book edition of *The Cloud,* 1973, ed. William Johnston, p. 93).

[4]I believe the Spirit is moving people to recognize and respond to this need. Retreat houses are flourishing. In addition, a new Catholic religious community founded in Memphis, Tennessee — the "House of the Lord" — offers a "year of spiritual formation" to men and women whose desire is just to live a deeply spiritual life as laypersons in the world. The year is like a "novitiate" for people called, not to priesthood or religious life, but to lay holiness: to the task of embodying the Gospel in the ordinary circumstances of family and social life, of business and civic involvement. Its purpose is to form them in the understanding and practice of lay spirituality.

For other suggestions about how to achieve this withdrawal without interrupting the normal course of one's family or professional life, see my book *Lift Up Your Eyes To The Mountain,* chapters four and five (Dimension Books, 1981).

[5]See Catherine Doherty's classic book *Poustinia* for the theory and practice — and fruits — of individual days of hermitage (Ave Maria Press, 1975).

## CHAPTER SIX: ACCEPTING PRAYER AS A NORMAL PART OF LIFE — *Matthew* 4:12-16

*Summary:*

1. What Jesus teaches us as "Master of the Way" is truth that that can only be absorbed and appropriated in prayer. Consequently, to accept Jesus means to accept prayer as a regular, significant element in our lives.
2. This prayer is the prayer of discipleship; i.e., prayer that is designed to be a guidance system for our attitudes, values and choices. Prayerful reflection on Scripture is the normal method for the prayer of discipleship.
3. In order to reflect and pray over the words of Jesus, we need to schedule times and periods of "withdrawal" in our life. When we withdraw from all that is darkness and distraction

in our lives, the light of Christ can illuminate our minds through His words.

*Questions for prayer and discussion:*

1. What personal insights have I had into the meaning or application of Christ's words? What have I seen that I was not taught? When and how did I get these insights? Have I shared them with anyone?
2. What is it in my life that lets me qualify as a disciple — i.e., a student — of Jesus Christ? When and how do I study or reflect on His words? Is personal learning from Jesus a significant part of my life? What form does it take?
3. What opportunities are available to me for withdrawal in solitude and prayer? Do I have a "quiet place" at home to which I can go? When is this available to me? Is there any other place where I can be alone and undisturbed for reflection and prayer? Do I ever make weekend retreats? Where could I make one?

## CHAPTER SEVEN

## ACCEPTING CHOICES AS
## THE EXPRESSION OF RESPONSE

The people who study these things tell us that eighty percent of human communication is nonverbal. And certainly a great deal of what we learn comes to us, not through hearing but through doing. It would be strange, then, if Jesus, the "Master of the Way," did not teach us by calling on us to act.

And, as a matter of fact, in the very first initiative that Matthew reports of Jesus' public ministry, we find Him teaching through what He calls on people to do.

Jesus is walking along the shore of Lake Gennesaret (more commonly called the Sea of Galilee). He sees two brothers casting a net into the sea. Their names are Simon and Andrew. "Come follow me," He says to them, "and I will make you fishers of men." At this, the Gospel tells us, "they immediately abandoned their nets and became his followers" (see *Matthew* 4:18-20).

He repeats the same scene a little farther along the shore with two other brothers, James and John, who are working with their father. At Jesus' invitation they immediately "abandoned boat and father to follow him."

Jesus is teaching them here — and through them teaching us — a fundamental principle of all life based on faith in Him. It is this: that our words, and especially our words of faith, have only the value of our actions. If we want to know that we believe in Him, that our faith is real, we must experience our faith by expressing it. What we are willing to do for Him is the measure of how much we believe.

Jesus is not an academic teacher. The "way" that He is Master of is the way of life. For that reason, we have learned nothing from Jesus until we begin to live it. And He makes this clear through the very first people He calls.

From the point of view of teaching, the important element in this story is not the promise Jesus makes to the brothers, but the act He calls on them to perform as a proof that they believe in it.

He has promised them transcendent purpose and meaning in life: "I will make you fishers of men." The value of their work and of their lives will no longer be limited to the immediate — and transitory — effects they are able to bring about through their actions on this earth. The fish people catch are soon eaten, or they spoil. The books people write are soon forgotten, or their readers die. The lives people save will end in a few years anyway. Even the cities people build and the nations they found will eventually crumble. But if we are able — through our work of catching fish, of writing books, of healing bodies or building cities — to help people in any way to know and love God better, then in these works we are "fishers of men." And the effect of our lives will last forever. This is the promise Jesus made to His disciples, and it is the promise He makes to us. The question is, do we believe it? For it is only in believing it that we are able to accept Jesus as the Teacher and transformer of life that He is.[1]

When Jesus makes this promise to the brothers on the shore of Lake Gennesaret, He teaches them at the same time how to respond to it. So that they will know that they do in fact believe in His promise, that they do accept it as real, Jesus calls on them to leave, to abandon, all that gives purpose and meaning to their lives right now. Like Abraham who left his "country, his kinsfolk and his father's house" as a proof of belief in God's promise to him (see *Genesis* 12:1, ff. and above, ch. 1, p. 7 ff.), the disciples "abandoned boat and father to follow him." They left behind their work, their means of livelihood, and their family connections. It was in the act of doing this that they knew they believed in Him.

We have already seen this principle appearing in the preaching of John the Baptizer. He urges those who intend to listen to his call to conversion to "bring forth fruits" worthy of the repentance they profess. A true Christian conversion should be expressed in deeds that are real, radical and unambiguously motivated by faith (see chapter one, above).

And now, before Jesus even begins to preach, He re-emphasizes the same principle. Response to Him is made in action, not in breath alone. We know we believe in His words, in His promise, in His individual call to each one of us when we find ourselves investing what is most precious to us in our response to His inspirations, His words.

Christianity is a religion of choices. Its emphasis is not on what one knows, but on how one responds to what one knows. It is true Jesus said, "Eternal life is this: to *know* you, the only true God, and him whom you have sent, Jesus Christ" *(John* 17:3). But in the Hebrew of the Bible, to "know" someone means to be in a living, personal relationship with him. The reality we "know" in the Scriptural sense is the reality we have concrete experience of. And we have no real, no concrete experience of God as He really is in our lives until we *respond* to His reality (and to His revelation, if we are to know the Christian God) with actions and choices that engage our very life.[2]

If we wish to be disciples of Jesus, then, we must come to Him prepared to respond to His teaching with choices. And those choices will concern, not just the marginal areas of our lives, like what we do on Sunday mornings, or the kind of prayers we say, but the stance we take toward the use of existence itself.

We will have to decide what value we place on our lives in this world, where that value comes from, and how it can best be brought to its fullness. And we will have to translate these decisions into concrete choices that affect our work, our lifestyle, our social relationships, our goals and priorities in life, our use of time and money.

Jesus is the Teacher of life, the "Master of the Way." We cannot accept Him as this unless we are willing to translate our acceptance into real, concrete decisions that affect the way we live. When Jesus summons us to faith in Himself, He summons us at the same time to choices that express that faith — choices which could have no meaning or motivation except through faith in Him.

Accepting Jesus, then, is not an academic act, a purely intellectual response. It is an act of taking possession of our own being through a deep appropriation of our power of free choice. To accept Jesus is to become a person free and bold enough to express response to Him in choices that engage the very roots of our life and activity on earth. We accept Jesus in an act of gathering our whole life together and pushing it across the table toward Him. If this appears to be a gamble, it is a gamble whose stakes are so high that in the act of making the gamble we know we are not gambling but sure. No one would rationally risk what we are called upon to risk in following Jesus. If we are willing to make the choices that seem to involve this risk — the risk of all our meaning and fulfillment in life — it must be we are sure. And that surety — no matter how much fear and doubt may accompany it on the emotional or psychological level — is the experience of faith.

If we are ready to take possession of our being in this sense, to take responsibility for our lives by acknowledging and using the ability we have to respond with free choices to the challenge of existence, then we are ready to listen to Jesus. We are ready to hear His challenge.

If this readiness is ours, we are prepared to hear Jesus teaching in the Sermon on the Mount.

### FOOTNOTES

[1]For the content of this promise, and the way Jesus gives transcendent meaning and value to the work and the lives of all who follow Him, see my previous book: *Questions For Today: WHY JESUS?* chapter two: "Jesus Is Meaning In Life" (Dimension Books, 1981).

[2]See Xaviet Leon-Dufour: *Dictionary of Biblical Theology* (Seabury Press, 1978) under "know," and *The Interpreter's Dictionary of the Bible,* ed. George Buttrick *et al.,* (Abingdon Press, 1962) under "knowledge."

## CHAPTER SEVEN: ACCEPTING CHOICES AS
## THE EXPRESSION OF RESPONSE — *Matthew* 4:17-22

*Summary:*

1. Jesus teaches us through what He calls on us to do. And when we profess belief in Him He calls on us to express that belief in actions which would not make sense without it. What we are willing to do and to risk for Jesus is the measure of how much we believe in Him.

2. Our acceptance of Jesus, then, takes the form of choices which involve the direction of our lives. To accept Jesus we must be willing to take possession of our lives and of our freedom and activate both as the expression of our response to Him.

*Questions for prayer and discussion:*

1. Do I understand my religion as a religion of choices? What else might it be? Is there such a thing as Christian "enlightenment" which does not involve choice?

2. Have I experienced my response to Jesus Christ requiring me to enter into a stronger, more conscious possession of my human powers? Has my exercise of *freedom,* for example, reached new dimensions through my response to Christ? When? How? In what decisions or choices? What other human powers has my response to Christ required me to activate and to own?

3. What concrete decisions or choices have I made which prove to me that I believe in Jesus? What promises of His do these choices express belief in? Are there any promises Christ made which I am not risking anything on? How real are these promises to me?

# CHAPTER EIGHT

## TURNING VALUES UPSIDE DOWN

In the Sermon on the Mount *(Matthew* chapters 5-7) Matthew shows us Jesus the Teacher giving formal instruction for the first time. In this first "discourse section" of his Gospel[1] Matthew presents us with a composite picture of the attitudes and values Jesus taught in the beginning of His ministry. These are Christ's general instructions on how to live. Later on, as His followers become able to understand more, Jesus will go more deeply into some questions and reveal some even more challenging ideals. But already the Sermon on the Mount contains in germ the whole of His practical teaching. And it is revolutionary: it lifts up our vision to a level of attitudes and behavior proper to God alone. The Sermon on the Mount simply turns all previous attitudes and values upside down. It takes us so far beyond the good moral teachings of the past that they become, for all practical purposes, irrelevant.

The Sermon begins with the "beatitudes" — seven short statements which call for an "about face" in our judgment of what it means to be blessed on this earth.[2] Because they are such a radical reversal of the attitudes we are accustomed to live by, the beatitudes are able to alert us with a particular intensity to what we should expect if we accept Jesus as Teacher of life and "Master of the Way."

The beatitudes are basic to the teaching of Jesus, and they are a fundamental reversal of our spontaneous and cultural human values. Those things we take to be good fortune, those conditions we strive to realize in our lives, Jesus proclaims to be, not just unessential, but possibly even obstacles to our true fulfillment and happiness. As disciples of Jesus we should know that in accepting Him we are accepting a Teacher who will challenge the most unquestioned assumptions of our behavior.

We will look, therefore, at each of the beatitudes in turn, alert to the revolution they call for in our attitudes and values. But first there are two things to remark about the beatitudes in general.

The first thing we should be aware of is that for most of us the beatitudes are really not comforting. They are challenging. It sounds very soothing to say, "Blessed are the poor in spirit . . . Blessed are those who mourn . . . " if you happen to be poor or mourning. But if we really look at what these beatitudes are saying, it takes a great act of faith to find any comfort in them. The fact is, we do not want to be poor or sorrowing or persecuted. And there is no reason why we should, unless we believe in the rest of the Gospel Jesus preaches. In order to really rejoice in inadequacy, sorrow or oppression, we have to be explicit and firm about our faith in a way that very few people are. And we have to see the connection between these conditions which we naturally find abhorrent and the good fortune which Jesus associates with them.

This brings us to the second thing we should

notice, which is that the beatitudes are really not believable in themselves. There is no natural connection the mind can perceive between the conditions they describe and the happiness they promise. There is no reason on the face of it to believe, for example, that just because someone is sorrowing he will be consoled. Our human experience might well lead us to expect just the opposite. The poor are as likely as not to get poorer, and the sorrowing more sorrowful. Those who "hunger and thirst for justice" (as the old translations put it) seldom see it realized around them; and most of those who are persecuted — whether for holiness' sake or not — just continue to be persecuted until their oppressors get what they want.

It doesn't really solve the problem to say that the blessing part refers to the next life: that those who are poor, afflicted and persecuted on earth will be happy forever in heaven. It is not blessed to be sick just because someday one will get well. And the fact that one can look forward to eternal happiness in the next life does not make one "blessed" being miserable in this one.

What, then, makes the beatitudes credible?

The answer is: "the proclamation of the Kingdom." And this can be understood two ways.

One way of understanding this is to say that in the beatitudes Jesus is not saying it is more blessed to be poor, sorrowing, persecuted, etc. than not to be. He is just saying that those who are, as a matter of fact, disadvantaged on earth are now able to find comfort in the fact that some day their sufferings will be changed into perfect joy. This, as we pointed out above, is not enough to make one's suffering condition itself a blessing, but it is enough to let us say that those people who do suffer are, nevertheless, in spite of their suffering, blessed to be in existence, blessed by the fact of Christ's coming, blessed by the hope of eternal happiness that is theirs. What had to appear before Christ's coming as nothing but unmitigated bad luck now appears, in the light of the promised Kingdom, as a pain of short duration soon to be forgotten and swallowed up in joy.

This is a legitimate interpretation, because it is true. St. Paul is saying much the same thing when he writes to the Corinthians that it really doesn't make any difference whether a person is a slave or free, married or unmarried, rich or poor, because Jesus is coming back and "the world as we know it is passing away" (2 *Corinthians* 8:17-25).

Another way of understanding the beatitudes, however, is to go farther than this and say that there really is a causal connection between the condition each beatitude speaks of and the blessing it promises. According to this interpretation, it is a blessing in itself to be "poor in spirit," because this helps one enter into the Kingdom of God. It is a blessing to be sorrowing, because this opens one up to greater, more lasting consolation.

If we take the second interpretation, everything still depends on the proclamation of the Kingdom, of course. Nothing that is promised in the beatitudes can be believed in unless we believe in the action of God. It is God who gives the promised blessings, and He gives them as blessings of His Kingdom — or, in the more active sense, of His "reign" — which begins for each of us in this life when we surrender ourselves to Him, and continues into the next life, where our surrender to Him and our union with Him are complete.

What this second interpretation challenges us to do is believe that the blessings of God's reign over us are so great, even on this earth, and the conditions listed in the beatitudes are so favorable to our surrendering ourselves to His reign over us, that it is more blessed for us here and now to be ranked with the poor in spirit, the sorrowing, the persecuted, etc. than not to be. And this takes a big act of faith.

It is on the presumption of this second interpretation that we will now look at each of the beatitudes in turn, examining what they mean and why they are a blessing for those who believe in Christ.

*Blessed are the poor in spirit . . .*

The key to all the beatitudes lies in the first one: "How blest are the poor in spirit: the reign of God is theirs" *(Matthew 5:3)*.

In Scriptural language the "poor in spirit" were a class of people — the *anawim* — who were both materially poor and spiritually devout.[3] They had nothing to rely on except God. As a consequence they were most open to receiving from Him, and would listen to the news of the Kingdom most readily.

In our times we might translate "poor in spirit" as "those who know they haven't got it made." Those who are conscious of their own dependence, of their own inadequacy to supply all they need for themselves, are more apt to recognize the need they have for God. Those who know they are insufficient to themselves are open to something more. And that "more" can be the Kingdom of God.

Usually it takes some real need to make people aware of their inadequacy. And therefore anything at all which brings it home to us that we really haven't "got it made" — whether this be economic insecurity, physical sickness, social rejection, emotional problems, moral struggle, or failure of any kind — can open the door to "poverty of spirit." And this, in turn, can open the door to Christ and the Kingdom of God.

I once told a cousin of mine I wanted to work with the young. Nearing fifty himself, he advised me against it. "The young don't need what you as a priest have to offer," he said. "Or they don't think they do. They are the 'fatbellies.' They have their strength; they have popularity and talent and no obligations to anyone. They have their whole lives ahead of them. And a million different things they can do. They just don't know they have any need for God."

He went on: "Work with the people my age. When you're in the shape we're in, and you owe five hundred thousand dollars to the bank and they want it tomorrow, then you're ready to hear about God!"

He had a point. There are other reasons to work with the young, of course. The young have many characteristics that open them to the message of Jesus: their idealism, for example, and their generosity. But — typically, at least — being "poor in spirit" is not one of them. As my cousin pointed out: "How many rich, smart, popular, successful high school and college students do you see interested in God?"

I would answer, "Thousands — but not because they are 'poor in spirit.'" For that you need to have lived long enough or suffered deeply enough to know that you "haven't got it made." For this, age can be an advantage.

What we are really talking about here is not being in *control*. And nothing is more frightening to us. We want to feel that we are in control: in control of our health, in control of our future, of our jobs, of our economic situation, of our human relationships, of our own emotions and behavior. For us human beings, not to be in control of the situation leads to anything from uneasiness to panic, depending on how serious we perceive the situation to be.

But the very meaning of the Kingdom of God is that God is in control. The Hebrew notion of the Kingdom can be translated either spatially as "kingdom" or actively as "reign" or "rule." The core meaning of both translations is that God is in control; He reigns.

Jesus did not come to establish God's control over the political or economic situation on earth except indirectly. By calling all people into relationship with Himself — a relationship of discipleship and surrender — He does seek to bring all of human existence under His life-giving reign. Then He sends out again in His name all of His followers to live and act as His Body in family and social life, professional and civic life, and thus establish His Kingdom in every area of man's life and activity. But His Kingdom, His reign, truly begins for each particular one of us as soon as, and in the measure that, we surrender to the rule of His Spirit in grace; in other words, when we surrender the control of our lives to Him.

To give Jesus Christ control of our lives, this is what it means to enter into His Kingdom, to come under His reign. In the measure that we are surrendered to Him in non-resisting faith, hope and love, He can accomplish His full purpose in us. And He has told us what that purpose is:

> I came that they might have life
> and have it to the full.
> *(John* 10:10)

But for us to let Him do this, we need to give up control. And one of the greatest helps to do this is to realize how little we are in control to begin with. The poor in spirit understand better than anyone else how little they are giving up when they put their whole lives into the hands of God.

The feeling of being in control is an illusion any way. Jesus said, "Do not lay up for yourselves an earthly treasure. Moths and rust corrode; thieves break in and steal" *(Matthew* 6:19). He reminds us that none of us, by worrying about it, can add a single moment to our life-span *(Matthew* 6:27). The most essential functions of our bodies — our heartbeat and brain waves, for example, are functions we have no direct control over. If our very existence is a free, continuing gift from God, and we have no control over that, then we are clearly deluded if we fear to turn over to Him the control of everything else in our lives.

In the rest of the Sermon on the Mount, Jesus will come back to this theme: those who are able to become "poor in spirit" — to give up their need to feel that they are in control of their existence — will find peace in the security that God gives. They will experience already on this earth the happiness of knowing that He is providing for all their needs. And He will be able to lead them in fact into the fullness of life which is the blessing of His Kingdom.

Obvious as this is, it takes great faith to live by it. When Jesus says, "Do not worry," He is not saying: "Whatever you feel you need, you can be sure your Father in heaven will provide it for you." What He is really saying is: "Trust that whatever your Father provides for you is all you really need." And He

Himself set the example of carrying this trust through the experience of death itself.

This first beatitude is a summons to radical faith. It calls us to face and to embrace the fundamental inadequacy that is ours as created beings, our total dependence on God. And it tells us that anything which helps us to do this — even if it takes the form of sickness, poverty, failure, or oppression — can be for us a blessing in disguise. Our only true good is to surrender to God and to God's action in our lives. "Seek first his kingship over you," Jesus said, "his way of holiness" *(Matthew* 6:33). And anything which  helps us to do this works to our ultimate advantage. It opens our hearts to accept the reign and the Kingdom of God.

From all that we have said it should be clear that the beatitudes are not just a collection of homey, spiritual wisdom. To make them this, to reduce them to sound, insightful psychology, an appeal to the self-validating values of humility, gentleness and love, is to weaken and distort them. It is essential to remember that we are only blest in the conditions Christ describes because the Kingdom of God has come. Jesus has come as Savior and Lord to break the power that sin and death hold over our existence. He has come to "reign" — to exert His saving power in the world and to take over the government of our lives in the measure that we surrender to Him. And His government is power and life:

Here comes with power
the LORD GOD,
who rules by his strong arm; . . .

Like a shepherd he feeds his flock;
in his arms he gathers the lambs,

Carrying them in his bosom,
and leading the ewes with care.

*(Isaiah* 40:10-11. See also
*Isaiah,* chapters 9, 11, 32, 49)

Jesus comes to offer us the Kingdom, which is the fullness of life. And He gives us this fullness by uniting us to Himself (which is the meaning of "grace" — the "favor of union with God") and letting us participate in His own divine life as God. The condition for this participation in His life is that we surrender ourselves to Him, as members of His Body, obedient to Christ as our Head. Thus we enter *into* His Kingdom by entering *under* His reign. And this is not just an act of submission; it is an act of surrender to total union with Him, to live by His life as members of His Body, to be one with Him as the branches are one with the vine (see *John* 15:1-8; *Ephesians* 1:22 - 2:22).

This blessing, this fulfillment is so great that anything which disposes us to accept it — to give up our isolated, individual autonomy and accept to be members of His Body, subject to Christ as Head — is also a blessing, no matter how much we may be accustomed to thinking of it as a misfortune.

The beatitudes make sense, then, only if we know that in and through Jesus Christ God Himself — infinite Truth, Goodness, Being and Fulfillment — is offered to man now as an object of choice. The pearl of great price is available, rendering the possession or dispossession of all other pearls irrelevant to our fulfillment. True happiness is found through one thing only: response to Jesus Christ. And anything which helps us respond to Him is a blessing.

Hence Christ's coming has rearranged the priorities of this world. The Incarnation and the offer of the Kingdom have shattered our human value system entirely and built it up again with Christ Himself as the foundation stone and keystone of the arch. To pray over the beatitudes, then, is to ask ourselves repeatedly: "What do I believe about Jesus Christ? Who is He for me? What does it mean to accept Him as the good news of my existence?"

Those who are "poor in spirit" are most likely to find the answer.

### FOOTNOTES

[1]Matthew's Gospel contains five discourse or monologue sections in which Jesus is shown teaching or instructing His disciples extensively. These alternate with narrative sections that show Jesus going about healing, responding to events, and making shorter statements in answer to questions. These discourses begin with chapters five, ten, thirteen, eighteen and twenty-three.

[2]We are used to eight beatitudes. The third, "Blessed are the meek . . . " is considered by Scripture scholars to be an addition to the text.

[3]See *Dictionary of Biblical Theology,* under "poor" and *Jerome Biblical Commentary* 43:30, on *Matthew* 5:3.

### CHAPTER EIGHT: TURNING VALUES UPSIDE DOWN
*Matthew* 5:1-3

*Summary:*

1. The beatitudes are a reversal of our basic human attitudes and values. They are neither comforting nor credible in themselves, but only through faith in the rest of the Gospel Jesus preaches. They alert us early that accepting Jesus involves accepting a message that challenges our unquestioned assumptions about life.
2. The "poor in spirit" are those who know they haven't got it made. Anything that makes us aware of our own need and inadequacy as human beings opens us up to receiving from

God. The blessing of the poor in spirit is that they are open to hearing and accepting the news of the Kingdom.
3. To accept the Kingdom means to accept Christ's reign — i.e., control — over our lives. We fear to give up control, but the truth is that we have very little to begin with. We are radically dependent on God for our very continuance in existence. To give God control over the *way* we live is not the risk it appears to be. In reality it is the only way of security and of fulfillment.

*Questions for prayer and discussion:*

1. What deep attitudes do I have which are contrary to the beatitudes? Do I want to be poor? To experience my own inadequacy and dependence on God? Do I find the beatitudes a comfort, a challenge, or both? Why?
2. Why does belief in the Kingdom of God make the beatitudes credible? Does this also make them comforting? Why?
3. What is there in my life that makes me aware of my inadequacy? Of my need for God? Do I see this as being in any way a blessing? Why? What positive benefit can I identify that has come to me because of it?
4. Who do I know that I would consider "poor in spirit"? Do I see that person as blessed? Why?
5. What can I do to increase in my life the blessing of being "poor in spirit"?

# CHAPTER NINE

## ACCEPTING TO FACE THE TRUTH

The second beatitude is: "Blest too are the sorrowing; they shall be consoled." This beatitude speaks of those who accept in action to face their human poverty. The "sorrowing" are those who are willing to look at their inadequacy, their sinfulness, the precariousness of their very existence, and come to grips with the deep anxiety of their souls. Another translation calls them "Those who mourn."

None of us likes to grieve. We avoid disturbing thoughts; we turn our attention away from realities which upset us. We see no point in going into considerations which depress us, because we have no firm hope of coming out the other end any better off than we were before.

As a result we choose to live with a lot of subliminal pain and anxiety, and to skirmish repeatedly with our fears when they show themselves, rather than to face the thoughts that bother us in an effort to overcome them. We prefer deep anxieties with superficial anodymes to definitive confrontations that must end either in the life or in the death of all joy.

We try, in other words, to the best of our ability to keep out of the ranks of the "sorrowing." We can't really do it, of course, any more than we can avoid sharing in the objective condition of the "poor in spirit." There is too much real reason for sorrow in any human life for that. But we can avoid facing the things we have to grieve over: our failings, our anxieties, our woundedness, our illusions and the lies we tell to ourselves; the shortness of life and the fact of our approaching death; the problems and evil in the world that threaten all human expectations. In our refusal to face the sorrowful realities of existence, we can pretend that death isn't death, that guilt isn't guilt, that a boring, meaningless life is an exciting one, and that the little psychological games we play with one another are reality. We can just refuse to think about the deeper questions of life. We can distract ourselves by total immersion in work or escapist entertainment. We can take refuge in rationalizations or put up a front of resigned, philosophical acceptance. We can be laughers, libertines or stoics. And by doing this we avoid both the name and the blessing of the "sorrowing" as the term is used in this beatitude.

The two issues in particular that people seem to avoid looking at are: first, the question of ultimate meaning in life (which involves facing the fact of death); and, secondly, the reality of guilt and sin.

An enormous number of people seem to live as if the question of life's ultimate meaning were not even significant. They get up in the morning, go to work, come home and plunge into family life or recreation as if it could be taken for granted that all of this is worth doing. And when someone they know is faced with a terminal illness they keep pretending in conversation that it isn't true. To others they will say, "So-and-so is terminal you know"; but when they are talking with the person himself they just never refer to it — like ignoring an elephant in the living room.

If you ask people about the ultimate meaning and value of their own activity on earth, their answers show most of the time that they have never thought deeply about it. Like the cat chasing its tail, they can find some meaning in what they are doing only as long as they don't ask where it is leading.

So the last question anyone wants to ask in a sales meeting is "Why?" Why bother? So we exceed our quotas? So we break all records? So we become Number One in the market? So what? Is it worth it for personal affluence? Is there any real achievement involved?

Motivation speakers make a lot of money, because people in the business world need incentive. But if success itself is not worth working for, what is the motivation built on? And what, ultimately, is the value of success?

That depends, obviously, on what you succeed at.

If we accept Jesus Christ, we are accepting at the same time to ask the ultimate questions. The two future disciples who met Him at the Jordan River in the very beginning of His career found that the first words He said to them were, "What are you looking for?" What do you want out of life? What are you living for?[1]

Another reality we don't like to face is the truth of our guilt and sin. It used to be popular with psychologists to play down guilt — almost to treat it as if it did not exist. And there were good reasons for this; anyone who has counselled people either psychologically or spiritually knows how destructive a chronic, morbid sense of guilt can be.

But real guilt, guilt that is an authentic human reaction to the plain fact of one's actual sins, is another matter. This kind of guilt does not go away because it is denied. There is no relief from guilt that is real except an honest admission of sin followed by forgiveness.

If we cannot forgive ourselves, we have someone who will do it for us: Jesus Christ. And His forgiveness is an act that has substance to it. He doesn't just "forgive" our sins in the sense of changing His own or God's attitude toward us; He *delivers* us from sin. He takes the guilt and infection of sin out of our lives, out of our existence. He overcomes sin, not only in its guilt, but in all of its effects. When John the Baptizer first pointed Jesus out at the Jordan, what he said of Him was, "Look! There is the Lamb of God who *takes away* the sin of the world" *(John* 1:29). To overlook the sin of the world might be a loving act, one that God alone is loving enough to perform. But to *take away* the sin of the world is greater still. This is not only love, it is redemption. And that is what Jesus came, in fact, to do.[2]

No one can accept to encounter Jesus Christ without accepting at the same time to face deeply the reality of his own sinfulness and guilt. Jesus doesn't deal with images, neither those we project to others nor those we hold up to ourselves. He deals with persons. And He cuts through everything that stands between Him and our true selves. We may come to Jesus — to His word, to meditation and prayer — intending to remain wrapped up in the reserve of our non-commitment, determined to proceed with caution and to pass judgment on what we see and hear before we take the risk of uncovering ourselves. But we will find, as others have found before us, that before we can even begin our investigation we ourselves are already summed up and judged. Jesus is looking at our hearts before we have even introduced ourselves to Him. The eyes of Jesus see us as we are; and in His eyes we see ourselves reflected as we are. But at the same time we see something else: the light of His deep understanding, acceptance, sympathy and love. The only eyes from which we can keep nothing of ourselves hidden are the eyes which reveal to us the all-embracing, infinite love of God.

If Jesus requires us to confront the ultimate questions about life and death, and to face the truth of our own sinfulness as well, He also supplies the answers to any question He raises, and the remedy for any sorrow He activates. If He insists that we look squarely at the bad news that is within us and around us, what He Himself sets before us is the good news. The good news is Himself and His Kingdom. It is this that brings the blessing to "those who mourn."

What Jesus announces is that with the fulfillment of God's promises in Himself, both sin and death have been overcome. In His coming and in the inauguration of the Kingdom, there is now an answer, and ultimate consolation, for everything we can grieve over. The problem of life's meaning is resolved, sin is forgiven, guilt is taken away, and everlasting life is promised us. There is even a legitimate acceptance to be given, and peace that can be found, in response to life's worst tragedies. In Christ and through Christ all is restored and made new (see *Revelation* 21:5). He has triumphed. In answer to the evil of the centuries, the reign of God has begun.[3]

Jesus proclaims in this beatitude, "Blessed are

the sorrowing; they shall be consoled." Those who accept to face the questions which cause them sorrow will find their sorrow turned to joy. The darkness they enter into will be converted into light. Their anxiety will be changed into security and their fears of rejection into an experience of love. But the starting point for this process must be reality. Only those who deliberately face and embrace the reality of their affliction will find the enduring consolation of God.

There are many people — I myself have met many of them — who seem to be untouched by the deep problems and questions of life. Their marriages appear to be happy, their children well-behaved, their financial situation secure, their social life agreeable and satisfying. To all appearances they are well-adjusted and happy, comfortable with themselves, with God (even when they are unbelievers!) and with other people. They are at peace with the world.

But I always have the feeling around them that they are skating on the surface of life. They seem to live in a world where suffering, pain, self-doubt, moral perplexity and the burden of social responsibility are just not present. Whenever realities like these come up in their conversation, or such human experiences as death, guilt, anxiety and fear, their talk becomes academic. They speak of these things as if they were elements of some other environment, realities they have heard and read about, perhaps even reflected on, but never been touched by. From all they seem to be aware of, you would think they had no scars on their souls.

To some these people may appear to be the ones who "have it all together," the blessed ones. But when I am talking with these untouched residents of the Garden of Eden I can't shake off the impression

I am dealing with children — grown men and women who are still living in the nursery of life.

I have met religious people who reflect this same shiny optimism. They seem to float one level above the world and all its troubles, riding on a magical carpet of heaven-sent peace and joy. Before they were "saved" they had troubles; but now there is nothing but joy, joy, joy, joy, deep in their hearts.

I question how deep it is.

Jesus never said, "Blessed are those who are always on a spiritual high." He said, "Blessed are the sorrowing; they shall be consoled." It is possible to use either drugs or religion to just soar above the problems of life — which may explain why the drummers of an emotionalist, evangelical religion are able to claim so many converts from the drug culture. "They just substitute one high for another," said a psychologist friend of mine.

The religion of Christians is not dependent on suppressing emotional pain. Jesus in His agony in the garden (see *Matthew* 26:36-46) neither suppressed nor "rose above" His pain in any emotional sense; He simply endured it. He endured it with the strength of God, and He promises this same strength to us. And He promised that those who are able to face their pain and endure it will find comfort — not an anaesthetic, and not immunity to pain, but strength, patience and consolation. "Blessed are the sorrowing; they shall be consoled."

The meaning of this beatitude is that those who accept Jesus need not fear to look any reality in the face. There are realities which cause us sorrow and pain. But with His coming and the beginning of His reign on earth there is an answer for them all.

## FOOTNOTES

[1]*John* 1:38. See the development of this passage in my book *His Way,* chapter two: "The Person of Christ in Your Life" (St. Anthony Messenger Press, 1977).

[2]For the development of this, see my previous book, *Why Jesus,* chapter three: "Jesus Is Deliverance From Sin" (Dimension Books, 1981).

[3]My previous book, *Questions for Today: WHY JESUS?* develops the answer Jesus gives to the questions mentioned here. See especially chapter two: "Jesus is Meaning in Life"; chapter three: "Jesus is Deliverance from Sin"; and chapter eleven: "Jesus is Victory" (Dimension Books, 1981).

## CHAPTER NINE: ACCEPTING TO FACE THE TRUTH
### *Matthew* 5:4

*Summary:*

1. The "sorrowing" are those who accept to face the reasons for sorrow that are in every human life — both those within our hearts and those in the world around us. Those who face the reality of human sorrow with faith in the good news of Christ's reign will find consolation that is real, true and ultimate.
2. Two realities in particular that people prefer not to face are the fact of death, with the question it raises of life's ultimate meaning and value, and the reality of personal sin and guilt. For those who accept the coming of Jesus, however, death has been overcome, life has taken on transcendent meaning and value, and guilt has been taken away.
3. The "blessed" Jesus speaks of here are not those who seem to have no experience of interior pain, nor those who seem to be always on a spiritual "high." The sorrowing are not blessed by being able to suppress their pain or "rise above" it emotionally, but simply by being made able through faith to endure it, find meaning and value in it, and ultimate consolation. Because of Christ's coming, all things are able to work together for the good of those who love God.

*Questions for prayer and discussion*

1. Do I envy people who seem to have no sorrow, no interior pain and struggle? Why?

2. What "sorrow" can I identify in my own heart? How much is sorrow over the human condition as such? How much is sorrow over my personal failings and sins? How much is sorrow over the condition of the world and of other human beings? How much of this sorrow did Christ share during His life?

3. What consolation does the event of Christ's coming offer for the sorrows I am facing in my own life? Have I ever had the experience of confronting deeply in faith something I was afraid to look at and finding consolation through this? What gave the comfort or consolation?

# CHAPTER TEN

## ACCEPTING THE PRINCE OF PEACE

What is known as the third beatitude — "Blest are the lowly (or the "meek"); they shall inherit the land" — is in reality not one of the beatitudes at all, but a later addition to the text of Matthew's Gospel. It has been accepted as one of the beatitudes for so long, however, that we will treat it as if it were one. Even though it is not part of the Gospel, it is Scriptural. This beatitude is a quotation from Psalm 37, which reads:

> Yet a little while, and the wicked man
> shall be no more;
> though you mark his place he will
> not be there.
> But the meek shall possess the land,
> they shall delight in abounding
> peace.
> *(Psalms* 37:10-11)

The Greek word *(praus)* that is translated here as "meek" or "lowly" appears four times in the New Testament as an adjective, and eleven times as a noun.[1] The meaning is almost always peace and gentleness as opposed to violence. Jesus describes

Himself as "gentle" and humble of heart *(Matthew* 11:29). He enters Jerusalem riding on a donkey, as kings did when they came in peace (conquerors rode stallions). And when Matthew describes the scene he quotes *Zechariah* 9:9:

> See, your king shall come to you;
>   a just savior is he,
> Meek, and riding on an ass.

The word "meek" is also translated "without display" *(Matthew* 2:15, in *New American Bible)* because Jesus is the king who comes in peace, to win people through gentleness to a free acceptance of His rule. He does not come with an impressive, intimidating show of power as those do who intend to impose their rule by force. That is why He enters the city seated on a donkey, the work beast of the poor, instead of on a warhorse.

This same attitude is the one we are urged to adopt in our dealings with one another. St. Paul appeals to the unruly Christian community of Corinth with the "gentleness" (meekness) of Christ because, as he tells them, "we do not wage war with human resources." He wants to come to them, not "with a rod," but with "love and a gentle spirit." Even when Paul must speak forcefully he insists he does "not wish to intimidate" the community, and he is careful to "stay within the bounds set by the God of moderation" (see 1 *Corinthians* 4:21 and 2 *Corinthians* 10:1-17).

Paul recommends this same attitude to Christians who must correct or admonish one another *(Galatians* 6:1 and 2 *Timothy* 2:25) And he proposes this spirit of gentleness or meekness (that is, the avoidance of all recourse to violence, intimidation or

force) as a key to putting up with each other's faults
and living together in love *(Ephesians* 4:6). St. Peter
recommends this gentleness especially to wives who
desire to win their husbands to a better way of life,
and to husbands in all their dealings with their wives
(see 1 *Peter* 3:1-7).

Underlying this exhortation to gentleness is faith
in the power of God (see 1 *Corinthians* 3:19-20;
2 *Corinthians* 10:2-6; *Ephesians* 4:3-6). We do not
need to impose the right on people by force, because
the reign of God has begun. Jesus has come to set all
things right, to make all things new, to overcome and
break the power of sin and death over all mankind. It
is His fight, not ours, and the weapons of warfare are
His to choose, not ours. But He has chosen to use, not
force, but gentleness; to save the world, not by over-
coming it as we understand the word, but by letting
Himself be overcome. He triumphed through His
defeat on the cross. He overcame sin by letting sin
have its way with Him and do to Him everything it
desired. He overcame hatred by a love that could not
be brought to hate, no matter what was done to Him.
This was a reversal of human history. It was an act of
power like turning back the tide.

From the beginning of the world sin has multi-
plied through violence. One act of aggression brings
on a greater act, until the consequences are beyond
all measure.

When Cain killed his brother Abel he was ex-
pelled from human society. He became an "outlaw";
that is, not just one who has put himself outside of the
boundaries of the law, but one who by that same act
has put himself outside of the *protection* of the law.
Where there is no law, there is no civilization, no
society. And this leaves nothing but savagery, the

law of the jungle, tooth against tooth. Cain saw this very clearly. He protested to God that if he was banished from society, "anyone may kill me at sight" *(Genesis* 4:14).

In answer, God explained to Cain the dynamics of the blood feud. What would protect Cain was the fear people would have of retaliation if they took revenge on him. This retaliation would come, not from society as such punishing crime according to law, but from Cain's family acting out of a sense of obligation to avenge the death of one of their members. If one man kills another, the victim's family will kill in retaliation, not just the murderer, but also his wife and his children. And then the murderer's relatives will take their revenge on the revengers, killing not just wives and children but also a few cousins, uncles and aunts. In this way, as the book of Genesis puts it, "If anyone kills Cain, Cain shall be avenged sevenfold." The law of life in primitive societies is that violence puts a person outside the protection of the law. But if anyone takes vengeance on him because of that, that vengeance will bring on more vengeance until for every person killed there are seven more deaths to mourn.[2]

The multiplication of sin through violence doesn't stop here, however. As the story of Genesis unfolds we see Cain's son, Lamech, taking vengeance beyond anything his father ever dreamed of. Lamech boasts to his wives:

> "Ada and Sella, hear my voice;
>    wives of Lamech, give ear to my speech:
> I kill a man for wounding me,
>    a youth for bruising me.
> If Cain shall be avenged sevenfold,
>    Lamech seventy times sevenfold."
>                                  *(Genesis* 4:23-24)

And the infection intensified until, at the time of Noah, the wickedness of the human race was so great that God "regretted that he had made man on the earth" *(Genesis* 6:6).

God tried to start things off anew by destroying all the wicked in the Flood, but it didn't work. In a short time they were right back where they had been before. The violence which set brother against brother (Cain and Abel), and then set family against family and clan against clan (the law of blood feud), now sets race against race and nation against nation. The story of the Tower of Babel explains in symbolic form how division is the fruit of sin. The Genesis story begins with a world in which the whole human race speaks the same language. Here is the society which every totalitarian ruler dreams about: a people united in culture, customs and government; a single block of human force, apparently able to accomplish anything it sets its hand to.

This people decide to build a city with a tower so impressive that it will stand as a symbol of the people's greatness and keep them united forever. But because the Lord is not in their midst, their pride, selfishness and ambition cause them to quarrel among themselves. Arguments turn into fights, fights into riots, and riots into civil wars. It becomes impossible for them to work together or even live together. They must separate.

So the people divide up according to their factions, one group going one way, one another. It is just a matter of time before, in their separateness, with little communication between them and without writing to stabilize the language, each group will develop its own dialect, then its own different speech.

I saw the "Tower of Babel" dynamic worked out literally before my eyes in Africa. Passing through a native village I would ask my guide, "Why is that mud hut over there apart from all the rest of the houses?"

He would answer, "That's a man who didn't get along with the chief. So he just moved out of town."

In a few months there would be more mud huts alongside the first one. More people who didn't get along with the chief. Then one day the separate huts would all be abandoned, and only the original village left.

"Now what happened?" I would ask.

"So many people moved out that they just decided to go off into the bush and start another village," my guide would explain.

It would just be a matter of time before one village would be unable to communicate in a common language with the other. And, as a matter of fact, in the country where I was there were two hundred and fifty different languages, two hundred and fifty tribal factions. The fruit of the Tower of Babel.

Sin multiplies sin. We respond to the faults of others with violence. This violence brings on more violence. The response we make to injustice becomes injustice itself, and injustice breeds more injustice.

This is the world into which we were born. We see the pattern repeated daily all around us. People wage war over and over again to bring about peace, and there is no peace. Violence ignites violence, and violence destroys life.

Into this world Jesus comes with the declaration: "Blessed are the meek; they shall possess the land." To all human appearances, nothing could be farther from the truth.

Typically, the meek are the *dispossessed*. They are the ones who are exploited, robbed of their possessions, stripped of their land, forced to flee into exile. The meek inhabit the land that is left over after the strong and the aggressive have taken what they want.

It is a law of history that those who want land must fight for it. And what is true of land we apply to everything else: money, position, power, respect, honor, prestige, human rights. The meek have everything taken away from them. Only the violent can hold their place in this world.

That is the way we think, and that is the way we keep leading the world into more and more destruction.

What Jesus has shown us is that the only way to possess the land, or our lives, or our own souls in peace is to give up defending them with violence. Through His passion and death He has shown us the way — and the only way — to redeem the world. It is by suffering evil, not by retaliating against it.

We never seem to succeed in believing, in taking seriously enough, the message of Christ's passion. He came to be the Savior. But He chose a way to save the world that was the exact opposite of what all men expected. He triumphed by letting Himself be defeated. He saved by refusing to save Himself. This was a scandal to Jews and pagans alike (see *Matthew* 27:42; *Luke* 23:36-37). He even refused to save those who were crucified with Him (see *Luke* 23:39). He simply refused to accept the role of physical rescuer from evil. If this is a scandal to us, it was just as much a scandal to the men and women of His own time. The Jesus who was able to summon "at a moment's notice more than twelve legions of angels" *(Matthew*

26:53) to throw back the violence of His oppressors refused to summon them. And He refuses still. It is not with soldiers and guns and tanks and terrorism and all the instruments of technological warfare that the land will be delivered, but by the meek who know how to possess it — or be dispossessed of it — in peace.

We may not understand how Jesus can say that the meek shall "possess the land." We may not be able to see, in any concrete way, how this actually does or can come about, when the opposite seems to be the obvious fact. But we are able to see for ourselves that the violent, even when they have conquered and appropriated the land, never possess it. No one who is interiorly attached to anything truly possesses it. Those whose hearts cling to what they possess live in constant fear of losing it. Their possessions bring them no joy.

The beatitude, "Blessed are the meek . . . " may be, more than any of the others, an explicit contradiction to the spirit of our times. What we see around us today is the strong nations holding one another at bay by an increasingly terrifying stockpile of devastating weapons. Weaker nations align themselves with the more powerful ones to insure their own defense. And in the emerging nations one new ruler after another tries to perpetuate his power by creating a military machine obedient to his every command. Those groups who are not able to gain control of government resort to terrorism. Governments respond to terrorism with brutal repression, torture, and licensed assassination. The idea of possessing anything, or holding on to the possession of anything through meekness seems too absurd to even enter into political discussion.

And for that very reason no one in our society feels he can promise himself that he will possess his land, his way of life, or his existence on this earth for very long.

"Blessed are the meek . . . " is a scandal to the thinking of our times. But the fruit of our times' thinking is proof incarnate that violence is no alternative at all.

## FOOTNOTES

[1]See *Modern Concordance to the New Testament*, ed. Michael Darton (Doubleday, 1976), under "Sweet." This concordance is designed to be used with almost all of the modern translations of the Bible — *Jerusalem, King James, New American, Revised Standard,* etc. — so that, no matter how the original is translated into English, one is able to look up the texts under the word one is familiar with. I have also used for this chapter the *Dictionary of the New Testament* by Xavier Leon-Dufour (tr. Terrence Prendergast, Harper and Row, 1980) and the same author's *Dictionary of Biblical Theology* (Seabury Press, 1978). These books, especially the last, are priceless tools for study and reflection on the Scriptures.

[2]I have taken this explanation of *Genesis* 4:1-16 from Bruce Vawter's book *A Path Through Genesis* (Sheed and Ward, fifth printing, 1963), pp. 74-75.

## CHAPTER TEN: ACCEPTING THE PRINCE OF PEACE
### *(Matthew 5:5)*

*Summary:*

1. The "meek" (or "lowly") are those who refuse to use violence as a means to avoid suffering or to right wrongs. This is the attitude Jesus showed throughout His life, and especially in His passion and death. It is the attitude St. Paul recommends us to take in our dealings with one another.
2. Christian meekness is based on faith in the power of God. Jesus has come to begin His reign, to overcome evil and set all things right. It is His fight, not ours, and the weapons are His to choose, not ours. He has chosen to overcome evil by suffering its effects with love.

3. In choosing not to use violence against violence, Jesus began to reverse the tide of human history. From the day that Cain shed his brother Abel's blood, the history of mankind has been a history of multiplying retaliation and sin. Jesus broke the chain reaction by responding to violence with patient endurance, to hatred with love.

4. History and current experience appear to contradict the conclusion of this beatitude: the meek do not possess the land; they are usually the dispossessed. But in a deeper sense, only those who have detachment of heart can truly possess anything. The violent are never in peaceful possession of what they own, and their property brings them no joy.

*Questions for prayer and discussion:*

1. In what ways do the people of our times use violence to attain their ends (give concrete examples). How many non-physical forms of violence can I identify? Can speech be a form of violence? Silence? Social pressures? Economic sanctions?

2. What, precisely, did Jesus do to overcome the power of sin in the world? Did He do this to set an example for us? How can we work against evil in the same way?

3. Can I show from my experience of daily life how sin breeds sin and violence ignites more violence? How can we break the "chain reaction" of multiplying retaliation and injustice?

4. What ways of acting are there in my own life which are contrary to the spirit of this beatitude? How could I react in the same situations in a way that is gentle or "meek"? What do I think I would lose by this? What do I think I might gain?

## CHAPTER ELEVEN

## ACCEPTING THE BLESSING OF DESIRE

*Blessed are they who hunger and thirst for holiness...*

Hunger can be a pleasant thing, in measure. If our hunger is not too intense; that is, if we are able to call it simply "appetite," and if the prospect of satisfying it is close, our hunger just puts us into a state of pleasant anticipation.

When hunger is deep, however, and there is no prospect of fulfilling it, hunger is a pain. This is true of every hunger; not just hunger for food, but the even more intense hungers of the soul.

From this kind of hunger, the hunger of the soul, the only relief is distraction; the anaesthetic of escapism. To block out the pain of a hunger we cannot forget, we put ourselves on a non-stop cycle of work, entertainment and alcohol. We avoid being alone. Silence is like an immersion in flame.

For this reason, it does not sound like a blessing to us to have a "hunger and thirst for holiness." What hunger is more insatiable — and therefore more tormenting? And if we can take the words of the saints and mystics for it, the closer we come to true holiness, the greater become the hunger and the pain of our desire for more.

The "holiness" Jesus is talking about here is not just an absence of guilt, a state of perfect moral self-control. The desire that Jesus calls a "hunger and thirst for holiness," is something that we may not spontaneously think of as a religious desire. It is the deep longing of our personalities for perfect wholeness, the cry of our hearts for some kind of fullness of being. It is the need we feel to have our existence rounded out, to have some undefined, aching emptiness within us topped off — by what, we do not know.

Everyone experiences this desire — in some form, in some measure. Not everyone is able to call it by its right name — a desire for perfect wholeness, a desire for perfection in being, a desire to be filled with God. Most people, in fact, probably spend their whole lives trying to satisfy their desire with something it is not really a hunger for. Some think it is a desire for pleasure; others a desire for security. These pursue satisfaction through affluence. Others think a poor self-image is the problem. They seek a sense of well-being through achievement, or through finding personal value in themselves without achievement. Others think the ache within them is just plain loneliness, and they look for fulfillment through love. And many people know, or learn through experience, that it is not really a desire for any of these things. Having achieved everything they set out to achieve — except the satisfaction of their desire — they despair of finding an answer and just try to drown it out. Some do this by going crazy; others by going to war; and some by working their way to the top and just continuing to spin there.

Escape, aggression, and compulsive achievement: all are reactions to the fact that nothing else works. And so the greatest blessing of man's nature, his ability to encompass the infinite in desire, becomes the root of destruction. In his incapacity to find a remedy for his insatiable desire he tears himself and his world apart.

What Jesus teaches us in this beatitude is to call our desire by its right name. And as He teaches us to do this, He gives us assurance of relief: "Blessed are they who hunger and thirst for holiness; they shall be filled to overflowing."

The desire that we experience is not a natural desire. It is an experience of grace. There is within us, it is true, a natural desire for "perfect happiness." This is the desire of our natures as rational beings. And our intellects are capable of recognizing that no happiness can be perfect or all-satisfying for us so long as we remain on the plane of activity proper to creatures. As rational human beings we desire to know all truth, embrace all goodness, experience all being. But because we are creatures we cannot. Only God enjoys the fullness of total being, total knowledge, total goodness. To be "perfectly happy" as our minds are capable of understanding the term, we would have to share in the life, in the being, in the all-fulfilling experience of being God Himself. No human being — no creature — can aspire to that.

And so our natures are willing to settle for less. We could be quite satisfied not being perfectly satisfied. We would accept to be just happy, or sublimely happy, or ecstatically happy, without being perfectly happy — if it were not for the call of grace.

The fact is, we are drawn by grace. There is in us a desire which does not come from nature alone, a desire excited by a positive beckoning from God. This is a desire which will not be silenced. It cannot be satiated by any created pleasure or joy. Before we even begin to taste what is offered to us, this desire sometimes makes us keenly, painfully aware of how insufficient the present delight is to fill up the longing in our souls. This awareness can turn the prospect of a lesser delight into disappointment before we have even experienced it.

What this desire is, in reality, is our experience of being invited by God to share in His own life by grace. It is the inarticulate forerunner in our consciousness of the good news Jesus proclaimed in words: that the time of abundance has come. Those who desire have only to seek and they will be fulfilled (see *Matthew* 7:7-11). Jesus came that we might have life, and have it to the full *(John* 10:10). It is now not only legitimate, but expected of us that we should think in terms of being made perfect as our heavenly Father is perfect *(Matthew* 5:48). It is not possible for us to dream more extravagantly than God. As St. John assures us, "the One whom God has sent . . . does not ration his gift of the Spirit" *(John* 3:34).

It was this desire, the fulfillment of which he had already begun to taste, that made St. John of the Cross cry out to God:

> !Ay, quien podra sanarme!
> Acaba de entregarte ya de vero,
> no quieras enviarme
> de hoy ya mas mensajero,
> que no saben decirme lo que quiero.[1]

For John of the Cross the desire to experience total joy, the joy that can only be found through unreserved union with God, had become a positive passion. Every other joy, even the joy of spiritual consolations, just excited his thirst the more — so much so that he cried out to God not to give him any more gifts or joys or consolations until He came to give him perfect union with Himself.

John of the Cross writes from the heights of mystical experience. But it is an almost commonplace occurrence to meet people whose desire for the "more" is so intense and unrelenting that they find no satisfaction whatever in all that this world has to offer. The rich find affluence insipid; the sought-after find popularity a burden; the talented experience themselves as empty.

To such as these this beatitude is addressed. Those who hunger and thirst for holiness will be satisfied. At least, the beatitude proclaims, the satisfaction they long for is offered to them if they are willing to call it by its true name and pursue it. It exists. They are not, as some might be tempted to regard them, just unfortunate fools and misfits unable to adjust to the commonplace reality of this world. They are not a breed of Don Quixotes tilting at windmills. They are the chosen, the invited of God whose hunger and thirst is for holiness. And if they are able to believe in the proclamation Jesus makes here, and pursue the holiness He holds out to them through His Gospel, they will be satisfied.

This beatitude, like the rest, is a scandal to common sense. For us the normal, the reasonable thing to do is to adjust to this world as it is and be happy. What we desire for our friends, for our children, is that they should be content to get a job, find a husband or wife, fit into society, and settle down to a peaceful, mediochre life like everyone else. We feel it would be better if they just blocked out the nameless longing in their hearts for perfect wholeness. When the young are too idealistic, it worries us. We don't know what they might do. We don't mind if our "old men dream dreams," because we know they will never carry them out into action; but it does upset us if our "young men see visions" (see *Joel* 3:1) because they might be rash enough to try to realize them.

And yet, when we ourselves accept, even for a fleeting moment, to focus our gaze on the vision held out before us of soul-fulfilling joy, of perfect wholeness in grace, of absolute holiness, it is then that our vision is most true. St. Augustine expressed it years ago to God in the name of us all: "Our hearts were made for Thee, O God, and they shall not rest until they rest in Thee." God's response to this restlessness is given in the beatitude: "Blessed are they who hunger and thirst for holiness; they shall be satisfied."

If we accept Jesus Christ, we are accepting the blessing of a desire without limits that can only be fulfilled through Him.

### FOOTNOTE

[1]Oh! Who can heal me?
Finish giving yourself to me once and for all!
  From this moment on, don't send me
  Any more messengers
Who cannot say to me what I want to hear.
*(Spiritual Canticle,* sixth stanza: St. John's own explanation of this verse is given in his book with the same title).

### CHAPTER ELEVEN: ACCEPTING THE BLESSING OF DESIRE — *Matthew* 5:6

*Summary:*

1. The "holiness" of this beatitude is not just an absence of sin. It is a state of perfect wholeness, fulfillment and perfection that can only be achieved through total union with God. A positive "hunger and thirst" for such wholeness can be agonizing, because there is no way any human being can satisfy such a desire. Jesus proclaims in this beatitude that

the fulfillment of this desire is now available through grace.

2. Many people block out their consciousness of this desire. Or they identify it wrongly as a desire for pleasure, success, or human love. As a result they are never satisfied.

3. This desire is, in reality, an experience of being invited by God to share in His own fullness of life by grace. It is a forerunner in our hearts of the good news of Christ. To accept Jesus is, therefore, to accept both the desire and the path to its fulfillment.

*Questions for prayer and discussion:*

1. How much religion does it take to satisfy me? What do I ask of my religion? Of my Church? Is this all they have to offer?

2. What is the difference between "practicing a religion" and "leading a spiritual life"? Which am I doing? What is the goal of each?

3. What does "holiness" mean for me? In what concrete ways am I seeking it? Do I have a "hunger and thirst" for the kind of holiness this beatitude talks about? What do I feel the strongest desire for?

4. If I saw my friends, my children discontent to live the ordinary life of this world, and driven to seek a deeper, more all-embracing fulfillment, how would I feel about that? What would I say to someone who just could not be content to make a good living, raise a good family, and be an ordinary "good" Christian like everyone else? Do I myself feel this kind of desire?

## CHAPTER TWELVE

## ACCEPTING THE BOND OF
## GRACED RELATEDNESS

The first three beatitudes (excluding Matthew 5:5) teach us a radical reversal of our way of thinking about ourselves. They summon us to recognize and rejoice in our creatureliness, our inadequacy, our dependence on God ("Blessed are the poor in spirit"). They call us to face and embrace the things within ourselves we have to grieve over: our sins, our woundedness; our defense mechanisms; the fact of our approaching death ("Blessed are the sorrowing"). And they encourage us to acknowledge the passion in our hearts for perfect wholeness of existence, total happiness, absolute holiness ("Blessed are those who hunger and thirst for holiness"). These beatitudes turn our attitudes upside-down as we look inward toward our insecurity, our sinfulness and fears, our deepest inner emptiness.

The next four beatitudes deal with our stance toward things outside us.

The first deals with our attitude toward people in need "Blessed are the merciful . . . "); the second toward those things which promise to satisfy our own needs "Blessed are the single-hearted . . . "); the third toward people who are rejected or whom we are tempted to reject ("Blessed are the peacemakers . . . "); and the last toward the threat of being rejected ourselves ("Blessed are those who are persecuted . . . ").

All four invite us to an about-face in the stance that human beings spontaneously take toward other people and values in this world. As "Master of the Way" Jesus begins His teaching by calling us off the beaten path.

*"Blest are they who show mercy . . . "*

To be "merciful" seems a positive, an acceptable thing to be in this world. It doesn't appear so very contrary to the going values of our society. But this is only because the depth and breadth of Christian mercy is not taken into account in the ordinary use of the word.

To "show mercy" means to come to the aid of another out of a sense of relatedness. The Scriptural notion of mercy is rooted in the Hebrew words for "an inclination toward," for faithfulness to a covenant, and for entrails or a mother's womb. The mercy of the Scriptures, then, is a "gut" response, like that of a mother for her child. It is an inclination to help another that is based on a bond like that of blood relationship or the identification with another that comes about through a covenant of love.[1]

The "mercy" Jesus is speaking of is almost the exact opposite of that condescending benevolence which a superior being shows to an inferior. It is not the philanthropy of the rich who think themselves better than the poor — or who give alms simply to keep the poor at a distance. It is not the benevolence of the powerful who choose to spare the weak because it pleases them. It was his knowledge of this kind of mercy, and of its effects, which moved St. Vincent de Paul to say to the Daughters of Charity: "It is only because of your love, your love alone, that the poor will forgive you the bread you give them!"

To "show mercy" says more about one's attitude of *relatedness* than it does about the actual aid that is given.

That is why Christian mercy is a scandal. It is the one thing to help people — to help the poor, the unfortunates, even the criminal — so long as we retain the right to think of those whom we help as "them." It is quite another thing to come to their aid because we recognize them to be "one of us." The perspective is totally different.

It is not a human perspective. And this is for two reasons.

First of all, from our groundlevel point of view, those people who live reasonable, moral lives appear to be quite a bit "higher" on the scale of values than those who do not. The same is true of those who are educated, capable, productive members of society compared to those who are not. On our human plane of existence the difference between "high" class and "low" appears significant — just as, from the insects' point of view, there are such things as frail and muscular fleas!

From God's perspective, however, these differences between us are infinitesimal. Seen from the plane of His own transcendent height, all of us on earth are on the same simultaneously inspiring and pitiful human level. We are all simply creatures in need of His grace. As the pundit put it:

There is so much good in the worst of us,
And so much bad in the best of us,
That it ill behooves the rest of us
To criticize what's left of us!

Even without God's transcendent perspective, human sages can envision a certain leveling of humanity. Poets like Rudyard Kipling can remind us (with unconscious British snobbery) that "the Colonel's Lady an' Judy O'Grady/Are sisters under their skins" *(The Ladies)*. Robert Burns can take us beneath the "tinsel show" of rank and honors to see that "A man's a man for a' that!" *(For A' That and A' That)*. The French proclaim "Liberty-Equality-Fraternity" and the Communists preach a classless society based on the brotherhood of all men. But the flaw in any attempt to equalize society from a human perspective is that the individual's dignity is only raised or lowered in relationship to other human beings. And it is easier to "level" society by lowering our respect for those who are "higher" than by raising it for those who are considered "lower." A classless society as such does not give us any positive or absolute reason to show mercy to anyone. Cynicism, rather than respect, is liable to be the outcome. And as a matter of fact, the most determined attempts to achieve this leveling through human means alone have worked through class hatred and merciless violence. The French Revolution and the Communist Empire are outstanding examples of this.

What Jesus preaches is not class struggle or a leveling of society as such. He goes deeper than this. He preaches mutual compassion and mercy based on the bond of our relatedness before God.

From the Christian perspective, what gives us our human dignity is not the fact that we are no lower than anyone else, or that no other person can claim to be higher than we are, but the fact that in God's eyes (and God's eyes see only the truth) we are all equally precious. No reform movement can "make" us equal to others, because on the level of basic human value we are all equal to begin with. We are equally called, all equally sharers by grace, when we accept it, in the divine nature and dignity of God. We are all the flesh of Christ.

And this is the second reason why the sense of relatedness that inspires Christian mercy is not rooted in any human perspective. Christian mercy is based on the consciousness we have that all human beings are called by grace to be sons and daughters of the Father, brothers and sisters to one another. The dignity we recognize in every man and woman on earth is the dignity of the Body of Christ.

This means that Christians do not wait for reform movements to bring about social justice before they treat all human beings as equals. For the followers of Jesus, those people who have no political rights, who are poor, socially unacceptable, and apparently making no contribution to society, are just as important, have just as much dignity, and are just as deserving of respect, as the sociologically elite. The Christian washes everyone's feet (see *John* 13:1-17).

For the Christian, all equalities and inequalities (and they are very real) on the level of wealth, education, productivity, culture, and even morals are so secondary that they are irrelevant. They simply fade out before the overwhelming fact of what we have become through grace, because of God's love and mercy toward us all. Each one of us stands before God holding an invitation to the wedding feast (see *Matthew* 22:9). That makes us social equals in the only society that counts: the society of those God recognizes as His own.

The Kingdom, and the invitation extended to us all to enter it, have changed all human perspectives. On the sociological level all sorts of distinctions still exist between the rich and the poor, the cultured and the crass, the educated and the illiterate, the law-abiding and the criminal. But all of these distinctions have been superseded. They just don't count any more in terms of our fundamental relationship with each other. Whatever distinctions exist between "us" and "them" on any of these levels, they have been swallowed up in the consciousness we have of being all one, all related, all equal before God in our invitation to enter His Kingdom (see *Galatians* 3:26-28; *James* 2:1-6), all one with each other and with God in the unity of the Body of Christ.

We are all equally invited; and we are all equally incapable, by ourselves, of responding to that invitation. This binds us together on another common level: that of our equal inadequacy and need.

The invitation to enter the Kingdom, to become members of the Body of Christ and sharers in God's nature is pure, compassionate gift on God's part. None of us deserves it; none is able to deserve it. None is able even to respond to it without God's gratuitous gift of faith, hope and love. And therefore there is between each one of us and the neediest person on earth a common bond of neediness so deep that it overrules every other distinction. There is no more condescension between us than there is between survivors on a raft.

The mercy Jesus preaches is not the mercy of the strong to the weak or of the just to the wicked. It is mercy based on a clear understanding of the need all human beings have in common with one another as they stand before the reality of God and the demands of living "in Christ." It is an admission and an acceptance of our common creaturehood, our scarcely differentiated sinfulness, our shared inadequacy. It is mutual compassion coming out of the deep cry of our hearts: "You today; me tomorrow!" Like the servant in the parable, we are expected to forgive one another and have compassion on one another's needs because we ourselves are so overwhelmingly in need of forgiveness and compassion (see *Matthew* 18:21-35). In this kind of mercy there is no place for condescension.

### *"They shall receive mercy"*

When we experience ourselves being merciful to others in this way, we are experiencing a love that is divine. To love others, not because of their rank or status or accomplishments; not because of anything they are doing or can do for us, but just because they are human creatures of God, dear in themselves because they are dear to the Father; and because in addition to this they are loved by Him and called by Him to the wedding feast and to membership in Christ's Body — this is to share in God's own act of love. It is to love in a graced way, as participating in God's own infinite act of loving.

Through this experience we come to know the love God has for us. In giving His mercy, we comprehend the true nature and reality of the mercy we have received.

Before we can love others as God does, we have to be loved by God ourselves. And all of us are. But we may not be in conscious possession of the love God has for us. We may not "know" His mercy, even though we have received it. Even while God is loving us and accepting us unconditionally as we are, we may not be able to believe it. This is because we do not understand what such love is, or how it can possibly be. But when we experience for ourselves the reality of this love in the act of giving it to another, then we know. By sharing in God's own act of loving another, out of the bond of relatedness He has chosen to establish through grace, we come to understand the love He has for us that is the reality of this same bond. Then we know what it is to be children of the Father and to trust in His mercy and compassion toward us because of the strength of that bond.

That is when the truth of the beatitude comes home to us: "Blessed are the merciful, for they shall receive mercy." When we know from experience, in the act of being merciful, what the mercy Christ preaches actually is, then we know personally — because we have experienced it — the truth of God's mercy toward us.

### FOOTNOTE

[1]See Xavier Leon-Dufour, *Dictionary of the New Testament,* under "mercy" (tr. Terrence Prendergast, Harper and Row, 1980).

### CHAPTER TWELVE: ACCEPTING THE BOND OF GRACED RELATEDNESS — *Matthew* 5:7

*Summary:*

1. The "merciful" are those who come to the aid of others out of a sense of relatedness. They don't act out of condescension, magnanimity, or even just out of a sense of moral obligation. They act out of a sense of oneness and identification with those who are in need.
2. This beatitude is based on the Christian doctrine of grace and of every person's call to share the life of God in the unity of the Body of Christ. It is a scandal to our natural, human

way of dividing the human race up into "we" and "they" according to categories of race, nationality, family, social class, cultural or moral standards.

3. In the act of showing mercy to others as an expression of the graced, unconditional love which is poured out in our hearts with the Holy Spirit we experience the reality of this love. Then we know and can believe in the love God has for us, and we enter into conscious possession of the mercy we have received.

*Questions for prayer and discussion:*

1. What people or groups of people do I normally include when I use the word "we"? What people or groups of people do I think of as "them"? What is my usual, my habitual basis for thinking of people as "us" or as "them"? Is this the norm faith teaches?

2. What does it mean to say we are "brothers and sisters in Christ"? What makes us this? Is this a bond of relatedness that is as real as the bond of family? Why?

3. Do I act differently toward those I think of as being "one of us"? What will I do for one of these people that I will not do for someone I think of as being "one of them"? Is there any story in the Gospel that deals with this question? What is it? (See *Luke* 10:29 ff.). How can I apply it to my own life?

4. What would it mean, in the concrete, if I tried to look upon all people as members of my own family and treat them accordingly? What ways of doing this would be realistic and possible?

# CHAPTER THIRTEEN

## ACCEPTING THE SINGLE PEARL

*"Blest are the single-hearted; for they shall see God."*

We live in a world that offers much and nothing at all. Much to gratify us and nothing to satisfy us. But all that is offered has value, if we use it for its true purpose, which is to increase our appreciation of God.

Everything God made is good and useful to us — so long as we do not expect it to satisfy the full desire of our hearts. To look to any created person or thing for ultimate satisfaction, so that any act of desire terminates in that creature and goes no farther, is idolatry. It is also disappointing.

Even an act as simple as eating food is a form of unrecognized idolatry if we let our appetites end there. But this is almost impossible to do. Since we are intelligent beings, we know in the very act of eating that the decision to eat is a free act. We do not have to satisfy the appetite. And if we choose to do so, it is for a reason other than appetite itself. Whatever the more immediate reason might be — pleasure, nourishment for the sake of survival, or just distraction — our ultimate reason is always the same: we eat because we judge that in some way it will make us happier; if not in the long run, then at least for a moment or two.

But to let our search for happiness end in any creature, without going farther, is idolatry. It is to say — if only for that moment — that this particular creature will do for our "god." During whatever span of time we act for the sake of some creature alone, we are living for the sake of that creature alone. And this is to make it our god (see *Colossians* 3:1-11).

This happens when the created value itself is the answer to the ultimate "why" of our action. When, for example, we can give no further answer to the question "Why am I eating this?" than the good that we find in the food itself, we are making food the ultimate reason for our action. If, however, we can say "I am eating for relaxation. And I want to be relaxed in order to live my life more fruitfully, both for God and other people," then our "why" goes further than food. It reaches ultimately to God.

We don't have to think all this consciously, of course. We are speaking here of the motivation of our hearts, not of the conscious awareness in our minds. Jesus said, "Blessed are the single-hearted," not "those with one-track minds."

St. Paul says of those whose hearts are set on the things of this world, "Their god is their belly" *(Philippians* 3:19). But many people, as we have seen (see above, chapter five), make gods out of much higher values than their bellies: another person, a work to be accomplished, even some state of ethical or spiritual perfection to be achieved. It matters little what we set our sights on; if our aim ends in any created thing, person or value, this is idolatry. It means we have lost sight of God.

Jesus responds to this fact of our existence by teaching us to seek God in and through all things. As St. Paul echoed His teaching: "The fact is that whether you eat or drink — whatever you do — you should do all for the glory of God" (1 *Corinthians* 10:31). We eat for the sake of the body, but our bodies are given to God. The purpose of eating, therefore, is to make our bodies (and our minds) more fit for His service. And this purpose includes the eating we do for relaxation or enjoyment, or just for the sake of being with friends, provided we come away from it refreshed and more able to face the challenges of life.

What we say here of eating applies even more strongly to the more important activities of life — our jobs, our family and social life, the choices that determine our personal lifestyle. In everything we do our intention should be pure and simple: the service and glory of God.

Jesus gives this teaching in several places throughout the Gospel: "You shall do homage to the Lord your God; him alone shall you adore" *(Matthew* 4:10); "your heavenly Father knows all that you need. Seek first his kingship over you, his way of holiness, and all these things will be given you besides" *(Matthew* 6:32-33); "The reign of God is like a buried treasure which a man found in field . . . like a merchant's search for fine pearls . . . " *(Matthew* 13:44-46). But in the very beginning of His teaching, in this beatitude, He says it with a promise: "Blest are the single-hearted, for they shall see God."

The "single-hearted" or the "pure of heart" are those whose motivation in life is unmixed: they seek only one thing in and through all that they do, and that is the service and glory of God.[1]

Jesus assures us that those who live purely for

Him will "see God." This does not refer to the face-to-face vision of God which will be ours in heaven. It means that if we seek God in all things on this earth we will find Him in all things here and now. Just as the idolatrous lose sight of God in their preoccupation with the things of this world, so those who live single-heartedly for the blessings of His Kingdom will find Him in all that they use and do.

Two statements are included in this teaching. The first is a scandal. The second is just a surprise.

The scandal in this beatitude lies in the exhoration to seek God and His reign over us in everything we do. This is not our spontaneous motive when we go about deciding such things as the work we will do in life, the man or woman we will marry, the house or neighborhood we will live in, the clothes we will wear and the car we will drive. We seldom, if ever, make any connection between these decisions and being helped to grow in surrender to God. We don't date for the sake of the Kingdom or seek a promotion at work as a means to get holier. We think that to try to make every decision in life a "religious" decision would be fanaticism — or at least take all the joy out of living.

And both assumptions would be true — were we narrowly fundamentalist in our understanding of what a "religious" decision is.[2] But if we are honest with ourselves, we will see that it isn't just narrowness and over-simplification that we fear; it is all-out love for God. We don't want to live for God alone. If we are going to live for any one person, we probably want it to be ourselves. Or someone dear and tangible to us, like our spouse or our children. But most of us probably opt for a fair and even deal: a good hand for our family and friends; a good hand for ourselves; and a good hand for God, with everyone sharing in the pot. We don't want to hand over the entire deck and just let the game be God's. Without really admitting it or calling it by name, we prefer to keep other gods besides Him.

In other words, in spite of what Jesus says and we nod assent to, we *don't* think we would be more blessed living single-heartedly for God and His Kingdom in everything we do. We think we are better off diversifying our investment!

If we understood and believed the rest of this beatitude, we wouldn't have quite as much difficulty accepting it. Jesus says that if we seek God in all things, we will find God in all things. We will not find less value, less joy, less fulfillment in the persons and things of this earth; we will find more. This is because we will be experiencing other people and other things the way they were meant to be experienced: as embodying the beauty of God; as speaking to us of Him and leading us to Him even as they lead us into a deeper and deeper appreciation of themselves. The joy of St. Francis of Assisi is proof enough of this.

The connection between seeking God in all things and finding God in all things cannot be explained; it has to be experienced. Those who have the courage to "die" to themselves and to this world for the sake of the Kingdom will find that they discover both themselves and this world on a level of value they never even dreamed of (see *Matthew* 10:30 and 16:25). But the proof is in the pudding. The reward of faith comes only to those who take the risk of faith.

The second statement in this beatitude is just a surprise to us — or at least, it may come as a surprise. Jesus teaches us that the way to find, to "see" God in all things is not through enlightenment of the intellect, but through purification of the will. We don't find God in the world by looking for Him; we find Him by living for Him. Just as the mystics who teach us the higher mansions of prayer spend nine tenths of their time talking about purification of heart, and only one tenth talking about prayer itself, so Jesus teaches us that the way to see God all around us is to love Him. This too is better learned by doing than by having it explained to us.

It is an axiom that love is blind. Passion blinds us. Whenever we are passionately fixed on any one person or value, we tend to be blind to everything else. And our being blind to everything else takes the thing we love out of perspective and so makes us blind even to the true reality of the very object our gaze is fixed upon.

This is true of every object but God. God is the only reality which must not be seen in perspective. To see God in perspective is to see Him entirely wrong. This is because to see something in perspective means to see it in relationship to everything else; but God is not in relationship to anything the way creatures are. God is outside the whole sphere of created reality; He is the Absolute, the Only One. Everything else must be seen in relationship to God in order to be rightly understood; and creatures must be seen in relationship to each other, because nothing in this world makes sense all by itself. But God cannot be understood as He really is except in the absence of relationship to anything else. This is because God was — and was complete — before anything else existed. All things exist for God, but God exists for no created thing. God simply is — and in the infinity of His merciful love He has chosen to be for us. If we want to see God as He is, then, we must see Him as He is in

Himself, and not through His relationship to anything else.

Naturally this is impossible for us while we exist on this earth. Only in the face-to-face vision of God that will be ours in heaven will we be able to see God in His absoluteness, as He is in Himself.

But we can do it now through love. We can set ourselves to loving God as the All, as the Absolute Good. And the way to do it is to bring this abstract-sounding reality down to earth and to focus our hearts on the warm, flesh-and-blood person of Jesus Christ, loving Him as He Himself said we should love God:

"You shall love the Lord your God
with your whole heart,
with your whole soul,
and with all your mind."

*(Matthew* 22:37)

If we try to love Jesus Christ like this, and to serve Him single-heartedly, then we will be enabled, as nearly as it can be on this earth, to "see God."

Passionate love for Jesus Christ is not blinding; it is illuminating. Through all-consuming, passionate love for Him who really is All we not only do not lose our perspective on the rest of the world, but for the first time we see all other things as they really are. To love God passionately is the only way to see God — or anything else — clearly. The abiding prayer of our hearts, then, should be for passionate love. And to accept Jesus Christ means to accept Him as the unique and single "pearl of grace price" (see *Matthew* 13:45-46) — as the all-embracing fulfillment of our heart's total desire. Until we accept Him like this we have not really accepted Him as He is.

## FOOTNOTES

[1]The "glory of God" means the greatness, the beauty of God made manifest on earth. Whatever we do that allows the grace of God to grow in us, to act in us, to appear visibly in and through our behavior is for the "glory of God." Jesus prayed on the eve of His death that He might be glorified in His disciples (see *John* 17:1-26). Through the visible triumph of His grace in them after the resurrection the world would know that His apparent defeat on the cross was really His victory. This same evidence is given by us today in the measure that we allow His grace, His Spirit to bring us to life.

[2]For some clarification on this point see my book *Lift Up Your Eyes To The Mountain,* chapters seven and eight: "The Desert and the City: Two Paths of Perfect Gift" and "How To Be An Ordinary Mystic" (Dimension Books, 1981).

## CHAPTER THIRTEEN: ACCEPTING THE SINGLE PEARL
*Matthew* 5:8

*Summary:*

1. The "single-hearted" are those whose motivation in life is unmixed. They seek nothing but the service and glory of God in and through everything they do. This single-mindedness is a scandal to our ordinary way of thinking. We think it would make us fanatics, or miserable, or both.
2. We are accustomed to serve and to seek many values in life — without integrating them all into one desire for the service of God. This is an unconscious idolatry. In the measure we let any value apart from God determine our life we make it our god.
3. The more we focus on any value on earth as if it could give us ultimate happiness, the more we lose sight of God. In the same way, the more we make God the goal of all our actions and desires, the more we find Him — His beauty, His goodness, His love — in all things. And it is only by seeing other things in relationship to God that we can understand and appreciate their true value. Thus the way to Christian "enlightenment" lies through the single-heartedness of will proposed in this beatitude.

*Questions for prayer and discussion:*

1. What motive or goal determines most of my choices? What do I daydream about? What determined the choice I made to do the work I am doing? To marry the person I married? To buy the last few things I bought?

2. Have I ever tried to bring all of my desires and goals together and integrate them (and myself) by focusing them on Christ? Do I have any goal or desire that I cannot follow out of love for Christ? Would loving Christ single-heartedly require me to give up the things I love now — my spouse, my work, my possessions — or just see them and act toward them from a new perspective? What would this new perspective be?

3. How can I do my work in such a way that it is totally directed toward the love and service of Jesus Christ? How can I live my family life in the same way? My social life? Would doing this increase my appreciation for my work, my family, my friends? Would I find more joy in them all?

## CHAPTER FOURTEEN

## ACCEPTING PEOPLE AS PRIORITY

*Blest too the peacemakers . . .*

Nothing in our times is more talked about than peace. And the only way we seem to know how to achieve it is by war. All over the world nations are arming themselves to the teeth for the purpose of maintaining peace. And the situation gets scarier and scarier.

We would except, then, that this beatitude would get an instant reception. To be a "peacemaker" should appeal to every heart. But it doesn't.

This beatitude, in fact, may be the one our society finds the least acceptable; perhaps because it is so practical. The choice to be a "peacemaker" is one which confronts us every day. It challenges our daily behavior in concrete ways that are too close to home to leave us comfortable.

The "peacemaker" is one who values human relationships — and specifically peace among people — more than any other created value. More than anything, that is, except God and relationship with God.

Jesus gives us some examples of the peacemaker in action later on in the Sermon on the Mount (see

*Matthew* 5:38-42). But here he gives us the general —
and scandalous — principle which underlies those
examples. We should value human relationships over
every other created thing. And therefore we should
not allow our relationship with others to be broken
off or diminished through any quarrel about money
or possessions ("If anyone wants to go to law over
your shirt, hand him your coat as well"); through any
excessive demands made on our energy or time
("Should anyone press you into service for one mile,
go with him two miles"); or even through outright
insult or rejection ("When a person strikes you on the
right cheek, turn and offer him the other"). In other
words, we should prefer — if we are "peacemakers"
— to suffer any loss of possessions, time or prestige
rather than allow our relationship with another person to be disturbed. This is radical doctrine.

In practice we do just the opposite. When we say
we want "peace," what we mean is that we want our
possessions to be undisturbed. "Peace" for us means
that our national honor is intact; that no one has been
able to insult us with impunity, and that no one would
dare to do so. Peace in the home means that everyone treats us with respect; that the husband doesn't
boss, the wife doesn't nag, and the children don't
make pests of themselves. If this "peace" is disturbed,
we will fight for it.

In other words, "peace" for us means having
things our own way, and we are ready to go to war
with anyone to achieve it. When we are self-righteous
about our desires for peace (as most of us are), our
defense amounts to saying that the only values *we* are
willing to fight for are values that absolutely must be
preserved. For countries this is the "vital national
interest." For private individuals and institutions, the

values are whatever they see as indispensable to their own particular goals in life. But whenever we are willing to give up our bonds of friendship and love with other persons — friends, family, business associates, other countries — because of any created value (anything, that is, which does not call into question our relationship with God), we drop out of the ranks of the "peacemakers."

No one would pretend that this is a simple principle to live by. It is not only difficult in terms of the sacrifice involved; it is also complex. There are times when we do have to go to court with our neighbor — not for the sake of our property as such, but because of our obligations to our family or to other people who depend on us. There may even be times — this is one of the most challenging, unresolved questions of our day — when a nation has to go to war. But according to the principle Jesus teaches, any recourse to anger, violence, or even to an argument which would threaten our good relationship with another is not to be accepted unless we simply have no other legitimate moral choice.

If we lived by this principle even half the time it would revolutionize the world.

One of the reasons we don't live by it (besides our basic, ordinary selfishness, of course) is that we have not understood or accepted that deep relatedness to others which we spoke of under "Blessed are the merciful . . . " In too many areas of life our attitude is still "we" against "them." We are fragmented into little pockets of belonging. We will foster relationships within our own group, and defend our own group (circle of friends, family, business, nation) and its interests against the rest of the world. But we do not extend this same sense of relatedness to the whole human race.

This is essentially the attitude Jesus was referring to when He said, "You have heard the commandment, 'You shall love your countryman but hate your enemy'" *(Matthew* 5:43). To "hate" just means in this context to look upon all outsiders (those who are not "countrymen," family, etc.) as the "others" and to fight them when necessary; that is, whenever their interests conflict with our own. With the "enemy" there is no bond of relationship to maintain.

But Jesus teaches us to do the opposite: "My command to you is: love your enemies, pray for your persecutors. This will prove that you are sons of your heavenly Father, for his sun rises on the bad and the good, he rains on the just and the unjust" *(Matthew* 5:44-45).

God makes no distinction between those who are His own and those who are not. All of His creatures are His own. He gives His love to all as indiscriminately as the sun shines on the whole earth or the rains fall on both sides of every border.

There is a tradition among the rabbis that when the Egyptian army was swallowed up in the Red Sea at the time of Israel's crossing (see *Exodus,* chapter 14) the angels burst into songs of joy. They looked up, however, and saw that God was weeping.

"Why are you weeping, Lord?" they asked; "Your enemies have been destroyed."

"Because," God replied, "the Egyptians too are my children."

When we truly accept all men and women on earth as our brothers and sisters — so much so that we value relationship with each one as much as we value it with our own family, and try to preserve it above all created values — then we will bear witness in action to that loving grace of God which has united us to Christ, to one another, and to the Father in the unity of one shared life. Our mutual love for one another as brothers and sisters in Christ will make visible the faith we have in our common adoption as children of the Father. Then the promise of Jesus will be fulfilled in us: "Blessed are the peacemakers; they shall be called the children of God."

Not only will our love be a witness to others of the loving grace of God that has made us children of the Father, but it will also bear witness to our own hearts that we have indeed been adopted as His children. As St. John wrote:

> That we have passed from death to life
> we know
> because we love the brothers.

(See 1 John, all of chapter 3)

The beatitude of the peacemakers is that in the act of living out their bond of relatedness with others they experience the truth, the reality, and the blessing of that bond of relatedness with God which has been given to us through our union with Jesus Christ. They know they have "passed from death to life."

When we accept Jesus, then, we accept that identification with Him as members of His Body which makes us true children of the Father — *filii in Filio,* "sons in the Son." We also accept a special bond of relatedness with other men and women as members of the same Body and children of the same Father. This relatedness embraces people of all races, ethnic groups and social classes. It commits us, in the spirit of this beatitude, to give priority to our relationship with others over every other created value. We are to love one another as we love our own selves *(Matthew* 22:38) as we love our own bodies *(Ephesians* 5:29-30). And we all know that we value the wholeness of our bodies and the integrity of our persons above all other things. In the same way we should value the wholeness, the integrity of our relationship of love with others. For each and every member of the human race is, or is called to be, a member of the Body which is our life.

Jesus came to share with us the life and the happiness enjoyed by God Himself. God's happiness, and His life, is to love. Since love is, as a matter of fact, the highest value in life, and loving relationship with others life's greatest blessing, the priority Jesus teaches here is indeed the key to the beatitude of the children of God. To accept Jesus is to embrace it as our own.

CHAPTER FOURTEEN: ACCEPTING PEOPLE
AS PRIORITY — *Matthew* 5:9

*Summary:*

1. The "peacemakers" are those who value human relationships above any other created value. This beatitude is in direct opposition to the prevailing attitudes of our society. We are willing to break up with friends and family, to sue, fight, or even kill one another because of property, prestige, or wounded pride.
2. One reason we fail to be peacemakers is that we do not accept in practice that bond of relatedness with others which comes from grace, from being all children of God the Father. We divide up instead into other groups according to family, nationality, social class, etc. We look upon ourselves as having little, if any relationship to maintain with those who are "outsiders." Thus we make distinctions between people that God our Father doesn't make.
3. Christians are called upon to look upon all other people the way they look upon their own families, and — as much

as possible — to relate to them in the same way. In the measure we do this, we bear visible witness to the grace of God that has united us all to Himself as His children, and to one another as brothers and sisters "in Christ." This is the way both to reveal and to experience ourselves as "sons of God."

*Questions for prayer and discussion:*

1. What persons can I think of with whom I am not in good relationship? What is the reason? Have I ever become distanced from friends or from members of my family because of a disagreement over money or property? Is there anyone I have chosen to withdraw from rather than risk another rejection? Do I avoid anyone because I value my rest, recreation, time or privacy more than that person's friendship? What would be a realistic way to respond to others in the spirit of this beatitude?

2. Can I see a difference in the way I react to the things that annoy me in strangers, or in people I work with, compared to the way I react to these same things in my friends or family? Would I feel the same way toward a prostitute on the street corner if she happened to be my sister? Would I judge her the same way? Would I do business with my brother the same way I do business with other people? Do I try to act out of the same relationship toward others that Christ has toward me?

3. What is my attitude toward violence? Can violence be verbal as well as physical? When, and why, do I resort to it? How often do I use threats, explicit or subtle, to bring about what I desire? In how many relationships with others is my goal to get the other to *do* what I desire or think he should do, and in how many is it to help him *become* interiorly someone who understands and freely chooses the good? Which is more important to me: that things should get done, or that people should live and work together in harmony and peace, even if it takes longer for things to get done, or they don't get done as well? Should I make changes in my priorities? Are there any issues or situations where I could realistically do this?

## CHAPTER FIFTEEN

## HOW TO KNOW WE LOVE HIM

*Blessed are those persecuted for holiness' sake . . .*

In none of the beatitudes does Jesus urge us to positively seek anything the world looks upon as misfortune. He tells us it is a blessing to realize the poverty of our existence (to be "poor in spirit"), and to face the sorrow that is within us ("Blessed are the sorrowing"); but He does not say we should try to bring more limitations or grief into our lives. And in this beatitude He tells us that persecution itself can be a blessing. But he does not tell us to seek it.

The blessing is not in persecution itself, but in what leads to it and what follows from it. Jesus says that those who are suffering opposition from others because of Him are blessed both in the fact and in the knowledge that their claim to the Kingdom is real.

In this beatitude Jesus is teaching a fundamental principle of Christian life in the world.[1] The principle is this: that for practical purposes, and as a general rule of thumb, we can measure our faith-response to the Gospel by the risks we are taking in order to be faithful to it.

The "world" as St. John uses the word in his Gospel, is hostile to the teaching of Jesus (see *John* 15:18-19; 17:9-19, for example). But the world even in a neutral sense, the good world of human affairs and culture, is always to a certain extent resistent to the values of Jesus — not out of any evil intention, but just because these values seem to call every human society out of its own orbit. When anyone, therefore, attempts to live wholeheartedly by the Gospel of Jesus Christ in the ordinary circumstances of family and social life, professional and civic life, that person is heading into conflict.

When this conflict reveals itself — whether in the form of insults, persecution and slanders (see *Matthew* 5:11), or just in the realization that one's stand on the Gospel may cost a heavy price in friends and money; in promotion, popularity and success — then one's faith in Jesus Christ also stands revealed. And so does one's hope and love.

The blessing is present already from the moment one takes the risk. It may happen that one actually loses nothing. One might even gain in every way: in popularity, in the respect of others, even in professional standing and economic profits. But all of this is irrelevant. The real blessing is that one has loved Jesus Christ enough, and believed in His teachings so faithfully, that one has been willing to risk the loss of something real and precious, just for the sake of living by His word.

Blessed are those who take this risk; they know that the reign of God is a reality in their lives.

It is not just a blessing to love Jesus Christ and believe in Him enough to take risks for His sake. It is also a blessing to know that one has done this.

Growth in the spiritual life is largely a matter of growth in awareness. Our relationship with Jesus catches fire, so to speak, from the moment we *know* that we love Him — just as our relationship with other people gains momentum in the same way. To believe and to know that we believe; to love and to know that we love; to place our hopes in the reign of God over us, and to know that we have placed them there: this is what we require in order to live a joyful, alive, and vibrant spiritual life.

After the apostles were scourged before the Sanhedrin because they refused to stop speaking of Jesus, we read that they "left the Sanhedrin full of joy that they had been judged worthy of ill-treatment for the sake of the Name" *(Acts* 5:41). No one likes to be persecuted; but it is a consolation to Christian to know that they have been judged worthy of persecution.

And therefore Christians never seek persecution. In fact, they should try to avoid it (see *Matthew* 10:23). But Christians do welcome the opportunity to take risks for the sake of the Gospel. When there is a choice between conforming to the standards and practices of our own close circle of friends and business associates, or of letting the ideals of Jesus Christ take flesh in our daily lives at the risk of personal loss, we welcome the opportunity to prove our love. At least, this is the attitude Jesus teaches. And in the measure that we live by it, we will experience for ourselves its blessing.

We might say that the blessing held out to us in this beatitude is "awareness." In the act of putting our lives on the line for Jesus Christ — or of risking anything else that is important and precious to us — we know how much we love Him. We realize how much He means to us. And, yes, we realize also how much we mean to Him.

It is no small blessing to know that we are friends of Jesus Christ. If we learn from Jesus, the "Master of the Way," how to come into this realization, we have learned a great deal.

To accept Jesus, then, is a blessing: it is to enter into the Kingdom of God. But to *know* we have accepted Jesus is an even greater blessing: it is to know that we have come under His reign. And that, Jesus teaches, is the blessing of those who bear witness to Him at their cost.

### FOOTNOTE

[1] I have taught it too, almost like a theme song. See my books: *His Way,* chapters ten and eleven: "Monk or Martyr: the Christian Choice," and "Martyrdom as a Milieu" (St. Anthony Messenger Press, 1977); and *Lift Up Your Eyes To The Mountain,* chapter seven: "The Desert and the City: Two Paths of Perfect Gift" (Dimension Books, 1981).

## CHAPTER FIFTEEN: HOW TO KNOW WE LOVE HIM
### *Matthew* 5:10-12

*Summary:*

1. Jesus does not encourage us to seek to be persecuted. But He teaches that persecution, when it comes to us because of our faith in Him, is a blessing. The blessing is not in the fact of persecution itself, but in what leads to it (namely, the faith and love which inspire us to risk the loss of real values for Jesus' sake); and in what follows from it (namely, the awareness that our faith in Christ, our hope in the Kingdom, and our love for God are all real — with the upsurge of faith, hope and love which follow from such awareness).

2. No one can be faithful to the Gospel of Jesus while involved in the ordinary human activities of family and social life, business and politics, without incurring risk. This is because the attitudes and values, the goals and principles of Jesus are not the same as those of this world, or of any human society or culture.

3. The blessing of persecution is present from the moment one takes the risk of persecution. Whether or not one actually does suffer the loss of property, friends, freedom or life, the expression and the experience of faith, hope and love are present as soon as one actually takes the chance of acting according to the Gospel at the risk of suffering loss. The more fear and risk there are, the more one realizes the reality and depth of one's faith, hope and love.

*Questions for prayer and discussion:*

1. Have I ever suffered loss because of my faithfulness to Christ, or to the way I thought the principles of His Gospel should apply to my life? What loss did I suffer? Did I experience any spiritual joy or consolation because of this? Any increase of faith, hope or love?

2. Is there anything I do — in my family life, social life, business (student) or civic life — that I experience as a compromise with the principles of the Gospel? What is my reason for making this compromise? Is it a sincere effort to live the Gospel prudently and realistically in this world, or is it just a fear of suffering loss? Does the decision I am following bring me peace and a sense of closeness to Christ, or does it make Christ and His Gospel seem less real?

3. How do I measure my "religion" — my love for Christ? Is it in terms of how much I pray? How much I "give up" for God in voluntary renunciation? How well I succeed in avoiding sin? How much good I do for my neighbor? Do I measure it at all by how much I *risk* in the decisions I make day by day in my family and social life, my professional and civic life? Do I think of holiness as being embodied — and growing — primarily in the *choices* I make all day long in my business and family life, in my relationships with friends and other people, in my civic and political options? Where and when do I have the most opportunity to show most realistically my faith in Jesus Christ? My hope in His protection and reward? My love for Him?